W9-AVR-122

PHILOSOPHY OF RELIGION

Thinking About Faith

C. STEPHEN EVANS &
R. ZACHARY MANIS

SECOND EDITION

IVP Academic
An imprint of InterVarsity Press
Downers Grove, Illinois

InterVarsity Press
P.O. Box 1400, Downers Grove, IL 60515-1426
World Wide Web: www.ivpress.com
E-mail: email@ivpress.com

InterVarsity Press® is the book-publishing division of InterVarsity Christian Fellowship/USA®, a movement of students and faculty active on campus at hundreds of universities, colleges and schools of nursing in the United States of America, and a member movement of the International Fellowship of Evangelical Students. For information about local and regional activities, write Public Relations Dept., InterVarsity Christian Fellowship/USA, 6400 Schroeder Rd., P.O. Box 7895, Madison, WI 53707-7895, or visit the IVCF website at <www.intervarsity.org>.

ISBN 978-0-8308-3876-9

Printed in the United States of America ∞

InterVarsity Press is committed to protecting the environment and to the responsible use of natural resources. As a member of Green Press Initiative we use recycled paper whenever possible. To learn more about the Green Press Initiative, visit <www.greenpressinitiative.org>.

Library of Congress Cataloging-in-Publication Data

Evans, C. Stephen.
Philosophy of religion: thinking about faith/C. Stephen Evans and R. Zachary Manis.—2nd ed.
p. cm.—(The contours of Christian philosophy series)
Includes bibliographical references.
ISBN 978-0-8308-3876-9 (pbk.: alk. paper)
1. Religion—Philosophy. 2. Philosophical theology. I. Manis, R. Zachary, II. Title.
BL51.E86 2009
210—dc22

2009026591

P 21 20 19 18 17 16

Y 26 25 24 23 22 21 20 19 18 17 16

To Charles Evans Jr.

And to Solomon Manis

Contents

General Preface

The Contours of Christian Philosophy series consists of short, introductory-level textbooks in the various fields of philosophy. These books introduce readers to major problems and alternative ways of dealing with those problems. However, they differ from most introductory texts in that they evaluate alternative viewpoints not only with regard to their general strength but also with regard to their value in the construction of a Christian worldview. Thus, the books explore the implications of the various views for Christian theology, as well as the implications that Christian convictions might have for the philosophical issues discussed. It is crucial that Christians attain a greater degree of philosophical awareness in order to improve the quality of general scholarship and evangelical theology. My hope is that this series will contribute to that end.

Although the books are intended as examples of Christian scholarship, it is hoped that they will be of value to others as well; these issues should concern all thoughtful persons. The assumption which underlies this hope is that complete neutrality in philosophy is neither possible nor desirable. Philosophical work always reflects a person's deepest commitments. Such commitments, however, do not preclude a genuine striving for critical honesty.

C. Stephen Evans
Series Editor

Preface to the Second Edition

It is difficult for me to believe that *Philosophy of Religion: Thinking About Faith* first appeared in 1982. I am very grateful for the way the book has been embraced and received by readers, having gone through many printings, with over forty thousand copies in print. The book has also been well received in the United Kingdom and has even been translated into other languages. As one can well imagine, the field of philosophy of religion has not been dormant during the period since the book was written. On the contrary, the past three decades have seen a vibrant surge of creative thinking about religious issues by philosophers. As a result, I have for some time been keenly aware that this book was badly in need of updating, but other scholarly projects made it impossible for me to do the necessary work. Finally, I embraced the idea of enlisting a coauthor to share the load.

I am very grateful that R. Zachary Manis accepted my invitation to do this work. Manis is a former student of mine, whose Ph.D. dissertation at Baylor University was partly a challenging critique of my own work, so I knew from personal experience what a good philosopher and fine writer he is. It is a great pleasure for me to introduce Manis to what will now be *our* readers. His major scholarly interests (like mine) are in philosophy of religion and Kierkegaard studies. He has already published articles in several scholarly journals, and I am happy that his first book will be coauthored with me. Manis currently teaches philosophy in the Courts Redford College of Theology and Ministry at Southwest Baptist University. He lives in Bolivar, Missouri, with his wife Lisa and two children, Solomon and Nora.

It is important for readers to know that this book has been thoroughly revised and updated. Although we hope we have retained all the features that made the first edition valuable, every chapter of this edition has been reworked. In addition, quite a lot of new material has been added. Here are some of the highlights: The section on the concept of God now includes a discussion of the problem of divine foreknowledge and human freedom. The section on the arguments for God's existence includes a discussion of the fine-tuning argument from cosmology. We now give consideration of the import of new explanations of religious belief from cognitive psychology. The chapters on objections to belief now include a discussion of pragmatic objections to religious faith. There is also a new discussion of the evidentialist challenge to religious belief, as well as of the claim of Reformed epistemologists that religious beliefs can be properly basic and do not have to be based on evidence. We have added expanded discussions of the relation of religion and morality, and the relation of religion and science. Naturalism and atheism have been given added attention, and the discussion of the problem of evil has been greatly expanded, now including separate treatments of the logical and evidential forms of the problem, as well as new discussions of divine hiddenness, horrendous evils and the problem of hell.

On these and other issues I have benefited greatly from the contributions of Zachary Manis, and I know that our readers will also find this to be true. The resulting product is a true collaborative work; each of us has revised and reworked material that the other author drafted. Manis and I are confident that this book will be a significant help to students and anyone else with a serious interest in the philosophy of religion.

C. Stephen Evans

1

What Is Philosophy of Religion?

Given the nature of its subject, religion is an issue of intense concern for every reflective person—whether one ultimately rejects its validity or not—because it addresses, and offers answers to, the most fundamental questions of human existence. Despite periodic announcements by "secularist" thinkers that humanity has finally come of age and no longer has any use for religion, most human beings are still vitally concerned with such questions as Is there a God? Why does God allow suffering? and What happens to a person at death? These and other questions posed by the great religions of the world are grounded in some of the deepest human desires, hopes and fears. Accordingly, religion has long been an important force in human life and human history, and there is every reason to believe it will continue to be so throughout the foreseeable future.

Philosophy of religion can perhaps best be defined, in a preliminary way, as the attempt to think hard and deeply about such fundamental questions as the ones just mentioned. In saying that philosophy of religion focuses on these questions, we mean, of course, to say that the answers given by various religions are also to be the object of attention. Philosophy of religion is therefore critical reflection on religious beliefs.

To explain why the focus of philosophy of religion is on religious beliefs, it would be helpful to say a little more about both philosophy and religion. Philosophy and religion are sometimes viewed as rivals, and the relations between them have not always been cordial. Some of the reasons for this mutual suspicion will become clear as we proceed. The questions What is philosophy? and What is religion? are surprisingly difficult to answer. Such complex human activities can be defined in many different ways. Indeed, it is possible to define "philosophy" and "religion" in such a way that they become mutually exclusive rivals. Religious believers sometimes have viewed philosophers as unsympathetic critics who try to undermine religious faith. To the believer, the philosopher may appear as a presumptuous champion of human reason who rejects divine wisdom. Conversely, philosophers sometimes have viewed religious believers as benighted defenders of superstition and blind obedience to authority.

While these kinds of conflicts have certainly occurred, and though tensions between philosophy and religion remain, it would be a great mistake to embody such oppositions in the very definitions of "philosophy" and "religion." Conflict is not inevitable. Some of the greatest philosophers have been religious believers, and some of the greatest contributions to religious thought have come from philosophers—religious and nonreligious. The question of whether religion is reasonable—indeed, the question of whether it should even try to be—is among the questions which philosophy of religion aims to answer. Such inquiries should not be settled in a peremptory fashion by the way we define our terms.

Religion is a complicated and rich human phenomenon, and as such, it is studied by academicians from many disciplines: historians, psychologists, sociologists, anthropologists and theologians, to name a few. Religion touches on the whole of human existence. A practicing adherent of a particular religion has not only certain characteristic beliefs but also characteristic emotions, attitudes and experiences. The believer usually associates with other believers in a community that may be relatively loose or extraordinarily tight-knit. The believer usually acts differently from the nonbeliever. He engages in worship and other religious exercises. He may attempt to follow a set of rules or principles throughout life; he may take as a role model the life of the founder of the religion.

Religion can by no means, then, be reduced to a purely intellectual phenomenon. A religion is not simply a set of beliefs or dogmas. Nevertheless, most religions at least include some distinguishing set of beliefs. A religious person does not merely have different feelings or attitudes or even actions. She *thinks* differently about herself and her world.* She worships as part of a community, and that community is defined in part by its beliefs.

It is natural for this "belief" element of religion to catch the eye of the philosopher. Philosophy has always been understood as a search for wisdom or knowledge. The philosopher is a seeker of truth; she wants to know whether religious beliefs are true and whether they can be known to be true or reasonably believed to be true. In considering these religious beliefs, of course, the philosopher ought not to wrench them out of context but to see them in relation to other elements of religious life. (Philosophers have not always followed this rule.) The philosopher's main interest, however, will be such religious beliefs as "God created the world" and "Human beings are destined for eternal life."

Philosophy of Religion and Other Disciplines

This focus on the truth and reasonableness of religious belief helps distinguish philosophy of religion from other academic disciplines that study religion. While the historian or sociologist

---

*In this book, we have chosen to employ the convention of using both masculine and feminine pronouns. We have done so out of consideration for readers who find the older convention (exclusive use of the masculine pronouns) disturbing, and we hope that any readers who might find the convention distracting will understand our decision to adopt it.

may also study religious beliefs, his focus is not specifically on the truth or reasonableness of such beliefs. False beliefs may be as important as true ones to the historian or sociologist who tries to paint a picture of the history of a religion or the place of religion in society.

The distinction between the philosopher of religion and the theologian is trickier. Theology is an activity carried on *within* religion (at least in theory). Thus, the theologian looks at religious beliefs from within, as an adherent or representative of a religious tradition. Philosophy of religion, on the other hand, as critical reflection on religious questions and beliefs, may be engaged in by thinkers who are not themselves religious at all, as well as by committed religious thinkers. (We will shortly deal with the question as to whether this critical reflection can and should be done from a neutral perspective.)

This initial distinction between theology and philosophy of religion is not quite acceptable as it stands, primarily because there is more than one kind of theology. What was said previously applies at least roughly to the theologian of an actual religion. For example, Christian theology includes the overlapping categories of dogmatic theology, biblical theology and systematic theology. A theologian who engages in any of these may in fact do some philosophy of religion, but that is not her main business. There is also, however, the kind of theology called ***natural theology*** (sometimes called ***philosophical theology***), in which the theologian attempts to say what can be known about God or things divine apart from any commitment to any particular religion, claims to special revelation and so on. Natural theology in this sense cannot be sharply separated from philosophy of religion, inasmuch as a good part of philosophy of religion consists in defenses of or attacks on natural theology. Still, the two disciplines are not identical, as can be seen from the fact that one of the issues in philosophy of religion is whether natural theology is truly vital to religion, as well as whether it can be successfully carried out. Philosophy of religion as a task will still be necessary even if natural theology is abandoned.

Philosophy of Religion and Philosophy

In addition to distinguishing philosophy of religion from theology and from the empirical disciplines that study religion as "factual" (history, psychology, anthropology and sociology), it is important to distinguish philosophy of religion from religious philosophies. To draw this distinction, a little more must be said about philosophy in general.

It is often pointed out by philosophers that the question What is philosophy? is itself part of philosophy. Philosophers do not agree among themselves about what philosophy is. Hence, it is probably impossible to give a completely neutral definition of philosophy, a definition which does not itself presuppose some philosophical commitments.

Some philosophers attempt to get around the obvious substantive disagreements among philosophers by specifying some supposedly neutral method of answering the questions of philosophy. This method can then be assumed as the common ground in terms of which philosophy can be defined. Unfortunately, however, there is almost as much disagreement about the proper method for philosophy as about the conclusions of philosophy. Rationalists propose that philosophy should restrict itself to a method of deductive proof, linguistic philosophers think philosophy should consist of the analysis of language, and phenomenologists argue that philosophy should concern itself with the description of "lived" experience. None of these methods really appears to be purely neutral, because, when unpacked, each invariably presupposes a particular view of reason or language or experience.

Perhaps a beginning can be made by noting what we have already claimed and what all the different schools of philosophy seem to admit: philosophy is a rational enterprise. Whatever else it may be, philosophy is a reflective activity; philosophy is a kind of thinking. Of course, not every kind of thinking will qualify as philosophical. No one would dignify one's thinking about what kind of toothpaste to use with the label "philosophy." The thinking we call philosophy is an unusually serious kind of thinking, directed to especially serious kinds of problems.

Certain kinds of questions seem to be asked by almost all human beings who have reached a certain level of reflectiveness. Who am I? What kind of a world do I live in? What is worth living for? These foundational questions have a universal significance, and they properly inspire the deepest and most rigorous kind of thinking. Answers to them, especially when those answers are comprehensive and organized, are called "philosophies." And the activity of seriously wrestling with these questions is called "philosophy."

Some of the organized, systematic answers to basic human questions have an undeniably religious flavor to them. In some cases, the answers are taken directly from a religious tradition. Other philosophies seem to have been developed in response to religion; they seek to answer the same questions and meet the same needs and therefore may be seen as rivals to religion. Both types of philosophies may properly be called "religious." Religious philosophy, then, is philosophical thinking which is religious in inspiration or direction.

Religious philosophy in this sense is not identical to philosophy of religion. As a form of reflection, philosophy is always self-conscious and critical. The philosopher not only builds systems of thought; he critically reflects on those systems. It is this critical and reflective side of philosophy that is most evident in philosophy of religion. Philosophy of religion is not so much religious thinking as it is thinking about religion, a thinking which can be carried on by both religious and nonreligious persons.

Can Thinking About Religion Be Neutral?

We have differentiated philosophy of religion from theology and religious philosophy by describing it as a reflective activity that requires a certain critical distance from its subject. In comparison with theology and religious philosophy, philosophy of religion appears to aim for a neutral stance. But is such neutrality with respect to religious matters really possible? Some religious thinkers have denied that it is, claiming, for example, that a human being cannot be neutral with respect to God. They claim that a person who is not properly submissive to God is, by default, in rebellion against God. "He who is not for us is against us."

Even more radically, one might challenge the assumption that such neutrality is even desirable. Might it not be that a neutral, disinterested posture actually precludes a deep understanding of what religion is all about?

Posing these questions puts us right into the heart of a central question in philosophy of religion *and* theology: the problem of the relation of faith to reason. One's view of faith and reason largely determines whether one sees philosophy and religion as inevitably hostile to each other, as coexisting peacefully but independently or as possible allies. Chapter eight attempts to deal with this issue more fully, but it is necessary for two reasons to say something about it at the very outset of a book such as this. First, some religious believers hold a view of faith and reason which claims that rational reflection on religion is impossible, useless or even harmful. In effect, they call into question the very legitimacy of philosophy of religion. Hence, some consideration of their view is in order if we are to be truly reflective and critical. Second, it seems only fair to try to become clear, and to help the reader become clear, about the standpoint taken by this book. What kind of thinking about religion is going on in these pages? We will approach this issue first (returning to it in chapter eight) by sketching two opposing viewpoints: *fideism* and *neutralism*. These we will criticize and reject. We will then propose an alternative that, hopefully, will preserve the strengths and eliminate the weaknesses of the initial theories. This constructive proposal will be termed *critical dialogue*.

Fideism

Many theologians have claimed that human beings are inherently religious. If they do not worship the true God, then they worship false gods—themselves or things of their own making. On this view, human beings are never religiously neutral; they are always *either* in faithful service to *or* in rebellion against the Creator. The faithful servant functions as she was meant to function and fulfills her created destiny. The one in rebellion, however, is always "kicking against the goads" (Acts 26:14). All her activities reflect the distorted and twisted character she has given to life.

Some have concluded from this that the thinking of the unbeliever is also twisted and distorted, either in all areas or at least with respect to essential moral and religious truths. Although the reasoning of rebellious humans makes a pretense of neutrality, this neutrality is in fact an illusion. Indeed, the very attempt of humans to think about God "for themselves," independently and autonomously, is proof of their rebelliousness. It represents an attempt on the part of humans to put their own thought and reason above God.

This view implies that human attempts to reflect on the truth of religious beliefs are disastrous. It is impossible for the unbeliever as an unbeliever to reflect on the reasonableness of religious belief and thereby become a believer. Rather, the unbeliever's only hope is first to *believe* and then, perhaps, come to see the reasonableness of the belief. If God in his mercy reveals to the unbeliever the truth about himself and the unbeliever, the unbeliever must humbly accept this truth. Perhaps God must "force an entry." The unbeliever's twisted thinking can only be straightened out as her status and life change from that of rebel to servant. Only the regenerate mind can see the truth.

This view implies that one cannot arrive at true religious beliefs as a result of rational reflection. The starting place for any correct thinking about religion is a genuine faith, a personal commitment. Fideism claims that faith is the precondition for any correct thinking about religion.[1]

Fideism puts its critics in an awkward spot, for all criticism of the view can be simply written off as the product of unbelief. It thus gains an invulnerable status against all attacks. But it gains this status at a rather high cost; the fideist cannot attempt to win over his critics by rational argument or even attempt to engage in rational dialogue with those who disagree. The presupposition of such dialogue and argument is the possibility of common ground, some point of agreement that can be reflected on or appealed to. But it is just this kind of common ground which the fideist denies.

The attitude of the fideist resembles, in an interesting way, the attitude of some orthodox Marxists, who dismiss the criticisms of Marxism made by non-Marxist economists, political scientists and philosophers. The Marxist reasons that these people are committed to the economic status quo and that their criticisms are therefore merely an ideological smokescreen which hides economic self-interest. If a Marxist holds to this position universally and in a rigid, a priori manner, he eliminates any true dialogue between Marxists and non-Marxists. The orthodox Marxist loses the benefit of criticism, which might enable him to improve his theories. He shuts himself up in a sterile "world of the committed" and thereby loses the chance to show non-Marxists that Marxism really does provide a superior framework for interpreting political and economic events. In the long run, his party-line theories do not develop, and eventually they are accepted only by those who find it expedient to do so, and by those who know no alternatives.

In an analogous way, the fideist also encloses herself within "the world of the committed," and in a similar manner, she eliminates the possibility of showing the nonbeliever the superiority of a religious worldview. But fideism faces an even more serious problem: Where should one place one's faith? To what should one be committed?

In effect, the fideist says, "Commit yourself and you will see that what I say is true." The problem is that many people say that, asking for commitment to many different things. One can demand commitment to creeds, books, churches or popes. Religious sects, political ideologies (like Marxism), psychological cults and non-Christian religions all make their respective appeals.

The Christian fideist may, of course, respond that there is an important difference between her commitments and those of all other faiths. She holds to the *true* set of beliefs, the *right* presuppositions. She can see the truth because she has been regenerated; she has the witness of the Holy Spirit. Of course, these claims may be correct, but how does one know them to be correct? Adherents of other religions can easily make similar claims.

It seems that, in a pluralistic culture, it is almost impossible *not* to reflect critically on where one should place one's trust. And even if it is possible to make a commitment apart from critical reflection, the existence of even one Jonestown horror would make it clear that it is irresponsible not to exercise critical judgment when asked for commitment. To the sincere individual who really wants truth, the fideist offers no help; she offers only another voice crying out in the middle of the modern religious babel.

Perhaps the mistake of the fideist is to overestimate dogmatically the impact of unbelief. For the moment, let us concede that most (or all) human beings are in rebellion against God. Let us further concede that this status impairs their personality in all its functions, including their reasoning. From this, it follows only that it may be difficult for human beings in this condition to think rightly about God. Their thinking may be harmed and limited in all kinds of ways, but it does not necessarily follow that such thinking is useless. After all, God remains God, the Creator, and he may well establish limits to the ways in which even a rebellious creature may run amuck in his thinking.

At the very least, it seems wrong-headed to conclude at the outset that human thinking about God is worthless. Perhaps this is a conclusion one might be wearily driven to accept, after many efforts, but even then it would appear that human thinking would have to have a certain competence *even to recognize its incompetence.* Such a negative result might, in fact, be a valuable conclusion, analogous to the wisdom of Socrates, who surpassed his contemporaries by recognizing what he did not know.

But what about the charge of the fideist that critical thinking about religious belief is impious or presumptuous, an arrogant placing of human reason above God? It would seem that whether critical reflection about religious questions is presumptuous depends chiefly on two factors. The first is whether God, if real, wants humans to reflect about religious truth. If God had forbidden humans to think critically about religious questions, then perhaps it would be impious to do so, provided one had some way of knowing about the prohibition. But we see no good reason to think that God wishes human beings to suppress their critical faculties. After all, our ability to think is a gift from God, and it seems proper to assume that this gift, like others God has bestowed, is intended to be used, if used properly. And it certainly would appear to be a proper use of reason, when confronted by a plurality of competing truth claims, to reflect on matters as important as religious belief.

The second factor that would affect whether critical thinking about religion is legitimate is the manner in which the thinking is carried on. Clearly, it is possible to think about God (or anything else) in an arrogant or presumptuous manner. No doubt much actual human thinking about God is of this character. But this is surely a temptation to combat, not a necessary feature of critical thought about religion. A person who sincerely wants to know whether God is real, who is willing to recognize her own inferior status in relation to God, if he *is* real, who recognizes the fallibility and possible bias of her own thinking, who understands that it is unlikely that she will be able to gain a fully adequate understanding of God, who is open to the possibility that her thinking may have to be aided by God to be successful, and who thereby does not rule out the possibility of a revelation—such a person's thinking about God would hardly appear to be impious or presumptuous.

Neutralism

The opposite pole from the fideist is the philosopher who insists that our thinking about religious matters must be presuppositionless. Neutralists, as we will call them, believe that our critical thinking will be likely to help us toward the truth only if it is completely impartial and unbiased. Thus, to think rightly about religious matters, we must put aside all our commitments—or at least those commitments that are religiously "loaded"—and adopt a completely neutral stance.

The neutralist claims, in effect, that to be reasonable is to think without making any "risky" assumptions. Two sorts of questions must be asked about this. First, if the neutralist is right, is it possible to think reasonably? Can human beings think in a purely neutral, disinterested manner? Second, is the neutralist right? Does reason require that one jettison all prior commitments and assumptions?

With regard to the first type of question, it is painfully obvious that human thinking is very much affected by all sorts of nonrational factors. Our thought is colored not only by our prior experiences but by our emotions, our upbringing and education, the ideas and attitudes of our friends, our historical situation, and a host of other factors. It is true that by reflection we can become conscious of some of these factors and negate or reduce their influence. But it seems unlikely that a person could ever do this completely. Indeed, it would seem foolish and unreasonable for a person to believe she has done this, for such a self-satisfied attitude would harm her chances of uncovering other nonrational influences. Thus, the proposal of the neutralist should not be accepted as a condition or requirement of rational thought. It can be at most an ideal that one should strive to approximate.

But, second, is neutralism even valid as an ideal? Is the neutralist right to insist that rational thought must strive to be presuppositionless? A full treatment of this question would require a detailed discussion of the central issues in the theory of knowledge.[2] Such an excursion into epistemology is hardly possible here, but it is necessary to say something about these questions, even if what is said is cursory.

A long and venerable philosophical tradition holds that genuine knowledge must consist of truths which are known with absolute certainty. We shall label this view *foundationalism,* using the term in a "strong sense," one roughly equivalent to what some philosophers term *classical foundationalism* because of the prevalence of this mode of thinking in early modern philosophy. (In addition to strong foundationalism, there is also a weak foundationalism, which claims that some of our knowledge is properly basic or foundational to the rest, but does not claim that this foundational knowledge is known with absolute certainty. Rather, our basic knowledge is seen as fallible, subject to correction and revision. Weak foundationalism is consistent with the approach taken in this book.) According to strong foundationalism, in order to know something, one must have a conclusive reason for thinking it is true. But of course, to meet the requirement, one must also know that this reason is a good one, and therefore one must know it to be true, which seems to require having a reason for one's reason. This threatens to become an infinite regress unless one knows some things directly or immediately, things which therefore can be said to be basic or foundational to knowledge. If this foundational knowledge is not really known but is merely believed or assumed, then the whole structure of knowledge becomes insecure. For this reason, the strong foundationalist insists that this basic knowledge must be certain. For any proposal to begin with unjustified or unproven assumptions, as the fideist recommends, is a recipe for disaster. Only that which can be recognized to be true with certainty, by a purely objective thinker, will suffice.

We have already discussed whether such thinking is really possible. We are now asking whether it is desirable even as an ideal. Perhaps one way of getting a handle on this question is to see how well the strong foundationalist ideal accurately describes the work of those in the natural sciences. Most people would agree that in the natural sciences, people are working toward knowledge in a rational manner. However, many philosophers of science today would question whether scientists follow the strong foundationalist ideal.

It is evident that scientists make some assumptions that are at least subject to challenge and which cannot really be proven to be true. They assume that nature is basically intelligible and orderly. A uniformity of natural processes and of experience is also assumed as a basis for making generalizations. However, in addition to these very general assumptions, it seems quite plausible to claim that science only progresses if more specific kinds of commitments are made. Thomas Kuhn, in his landmark work *The Structure of Scientific Revolutions,* has called attention to the way "normal science" depends on what he terms a *paradigm,* a basic set of assumptions which is embodied in the practices of a scientific community.[3] Kuhn argues convincingly that the acceptance of such a paradigm is not simply a matter of "checking it by the facts," as the strong foundationalist might wish to claim, since the basic paradigm beliefs have at least some bearing on what is to count as a fact and how the facts are to be described. As some interpret him, Kuhn goes on to make the extreme and questionable claim that the adoption of a paradigm is a nonrational matter governed by sociological factors. Even if one does not accept this extreme claim, Kuhn's work still implies that science, far from precluding less-than-certain commitments, actually depends on such commitments.

The history of philosophy also provides an interesting way of testing the claims of the strong foundationalist. Perhaps the philosopher who most rigorously attempted to follow this program was René Descartes (1596-1650).[4] Descartes attempted to realize the ideal of pure objectivity by methodically subjecting all his beliefs to doubt. By supposing that all his experiences might be dream experiences and that it was possible that he was constantly being deceived by an evil being of great power, Descartes rejected almost all his previous beliefs as uncertain. All that remained was the certain truth of his own existence, which he affirmed to be undoubtable as long as he was conscious.

With this slender foundation of "I think, therefore I am" *(cogito ergo sum),* Descartes attempted to prove the existence of God, the external world and his own, immaterial soul. However, almost no one today finds Descartes's arguments convincing. It seems evident, rather, that the eighteenth-century empiricist philosopher

David Hume was correct in asserting that Cartesian doubt would be incurable if attainable.[5] Rather than laying a foundation for knowledge, Descartes's universal doubt seems a sure road to unrestricted skepticism.

Critical Dialogue

What option remains? We have rejected both fideism and neutralism: the former because it precludes rational reflection, the latter because it places impossible demands on rational reflection. But there is something correct about both these viewpoints. It can be seen from our criticism of neutralism that the fideist has a valid point when he stresses that our thought is conditioned by basic assumptions and attitudes. And surely the neutralist has a point against the fideist in stressing the value of honest, no-holds-barred, critical reflection on our commitments. How, then, can reason and commitment be combined?

Perhaps the two can be brought into a happy, if sometimes tension-filled, alliance by rethinking what it means to be reasonable. Instead of seeing reason as presuppositionless thinking, suppose we view reason as *a willingness to test one's commitments.* Perhaps the fideist is right in claiming that it is impossible to begin without commitments; perhaps it is not even desirable. But it is a mistake to claim that commitments, even fundamental ones, are impervious to criticism and modification. Perhaps the neutralist is right in urging us to strive to rationally evaluate our commitments, to reflect on them critically and honestly in the light of evidence and argument. But it is a mistake to think that this process of testing can or should proceed from a totally neutral standpoint, the standpoint of a person without any convictions. Although any belief can in principle be doubted, we cannot doubt all our beliefs at once without undermining the possibility of overcoming the doubt.

How does one go about testing one's beliefs? Simple beliefs about particular matters of fact are subject to fairly direct experiential tests. More general and comprehensive scientific theories can only be tested indirectly. One looks for theoretical coherence, predictive power, the ability to illuminate what was previously unintelligible. Usually a theory must be tested relative to its rivals. A scientific theory that explains a great deal will be accepted, even if it faces serious objections, as long as there is no viable alternative. Sometimes the decision to continue to accept a theory requires one to discount or reinterpret what purport to be facts; at other times it seems more reasonable to accept the fact and reject or modify the theory. In short, the testing of theories is a complicated affair, requiring an element of good judgment as well as honesty and concern for truth. One assumes that experience is not infinitely plastic; some theories fit the facts better than others. But the process of testing is not one for which formal rules can be given.

The testing of significant religious beliefs seems to be a basically similar matter, although the kinds of experiences which are relevant as evidence are far broader. The testing of religious beliefs is, of course, likely to be even more difficult than the testing of scientific theories. The reasons for this are many, but they include the point with which the fideist begins. Few, if any, people are indifferent to religious matters. Since religion bears on a person's life in a far more direct and personal way than science, one can expect it to be correspondingly more difficult to reach agreement on religious matters. Common ground may be hard to find, and rational discussion may sooner or later reach an impasse where both sides say, "This is how it appears to me."

But though common ground may be difficult to find (or even impossible, as the fideist claims), that is no reason not to *look*. Each person is an individual and no doubt must make a final judgment about the way things "appear" to him. But to the extent that one individual has made an effort to engage others in critical dialogue, he is entitled to regard his commitments as no longer mere prejudices, but rather as convictions that have withstood a process of critical testing and are, so far, reasonable. In the process of critical dialogue, the individual attempts to think through the alternatives and the objections to his own view that those alternatives put forward. In the course of such a process, a person's views may be modified or abandoned. What survives is not merely prejudice or bias, but, subject to a continued willingness to test what appears doubtful, reasoned conviction.

Such a process cannot be guaranteed to work successfully, of course. Finite, fallible human beings cannot survey all the alternatives or assess those they do examine with total accuracy. And the process of reflection cannot be extended indefinitely. The purpose of our religious beliefs is ultimately to guide our lives; if a person spent all her time critically reflecting on her beliefs, there would be no point in having any in the first place.

Philosophy of religion is best viewed, we believe, as a process of critical dialogue. Obviously, each participant in the dialogue approaches it from her own, unique perspective. This means that even her critical reflections about her faith are shaped somewhat by her attitudes, basic convictions and previous experiences. In short, people participate as whole persons, not as calculating machines. But the honest participant does not shrink from self-consciously examining any part of what she brings to the encounter. No commitments can be regarded as "not up for discussion." And although it may not be possible to be neutral, it is possible for the participants in the dialogue to be honest with themselves and others. This honesty requires a willingness to see if the evidence really is best interpreted and explained according to one's own theory.

Such a critical dialogue is risky. Probably everyone has heard a story of a student raised in a strict religious environment who loses his faith as a result of the critical challenges he encounters upon his arrival at a university. But there is something unhealthy and even dishonest about a faith that hides from such a challenge. Can one really believe in God wholeheartedly and at the same time assert that one can only continue to believe by refusing to consider the evidence against one's belief? Such a belief seems perilously close to a half-conscious conviction that in fact God may not be real, combined with a wish to hide this truth from oneself. (Note, however, that an honest recognition of one's inability to properly evaluate evidence is not the same as a decision to ignore evidence. It might be entirely proper for an uneducated person to refuse to consider complicated, abstract arguments that would only confuse and bewilder him.)

A genuine and robust faith will not shrink from the process of testing, for it is confident that it will indeed pass the test. If one genuinely believes that God is real (or that he is an illusion), one will not be afraid to examine alternative views and listen to problems and objections raised by others. Through this process the believer may have confidence that her faith will be deepened and strengthened. Furthermore, by listening to her opponents and by looking for common ground on which to show them the superiority of her belief, she gains the possibility of making her opponents into friends and allies. Instead of churlishly telling those who have other views that they must begin by accepting her own presuppositions—an action which is probably not possible even if it were desirable, since belief is not usually under voluntary control—she attempts to find ground on which both sides are comfortable. The process may be difficult, and with some it is doubtless impossible. She must not allow her opponents to lure her over the cliff into the thin air of neutralism, where no living human being can stand. But the search for common ground is worth making.

In the following chapters we will look at the dialogue over a number of issues as it has gone on in Western philosophy, including the following: (1) whether there are any compelling arguments for or against the kind of God believed in by Christians, Jews and Muslims, (2) how religious experience is best analyzed and what we can conclude from it, (3) whether a person could ever be justified in accepting some person, book or creed as having special authority, (4) whether miracles are possible and under what conditions one might believe in their occurrence, (5) whether any serious objection to religious belief is to be found in the natural or social sciences, (6) whether and to what extent the existence of evil and suffering in the world count against the existence of God. Finally, we will return to the issue discussed in this chapter: that of personal commitment and intellectual honesty in a religiously pluralistic world.

Obviously, this part of the dialogue is not comprehensive, and it is not one that would suit every potential participant. The issues addressed are largely those that emerge from a serious consideration of the Christian faith, though many of them have counterparts for those who adhere to other religious traditions. Most of the examples will be taken from Christianity. Thus, this book will probably be of more interest to Christians and people seriously interested in Christianity than to those of other faiths. But as an introduction to critical dialogue about faith, it is better to focus on the faith one understands best. For most people in the West, that is Christianity. It is our hope, however, that as an introduction to critical dialogue, the book will be of value to those of any faith, as well as to those who lack faith in any traditionally religious sense of the term.

2

The Theistic God: The Project of Natural Theology

A belief in God or gods of some kind is central to the great majority of the world's religions. Obviously, then, two key questions for philosophy of religion are whether it is reasonable to believe in God and, if so, what kind of God should be believed in.

Concepts of God

Though there are a great number of views about God, which vary tremendously in the details, most views about God can be seen as falling into one of a relatively small number of types. *Polytheism,* the belief that there exists a plurality of personal gods, is common among tribal peoples and is clearly present in Greek and Nordic mythology. *Henotheism* also recognizes a plurality of gods, but the henotheist restricts his allegiance to one god, either because he sees that god in some way as superior to the others or simply because that god is the god of his own tribe or people. *Monotheism,* often simply abbreviated as *theism,* holds that only one God exists. God is seen as a personal being, supreme in power, knowledge and moral worth, who created all other existing beings out of nothing. *Pantheism,* often associated with some varieties of Hinduism and other Eastern religions but not uncommon in the West, holds that it is not ultimately proper to think of God as a personal being—or, according to some, as a being of any kind. Such concepts are thought to be too limiting for God, who must ultimately be understood as identical with nature or the universe as a whole. *Panentheism* says that God is not identical with the universe but must be seen as including the universe. The universe is in some sense God, but God is more than the universe.

These are the major views about God that are found in the religions of the world. There are, of course, many interesting variations on each view, some of which are significant enough to warrant a name. Thus, *dualism* can be seen as a variation on polytheism, the dualist holding to a plurality of only two gods, who are opposed to each other. (Usually one god is seen as good and the other as evil.) *Deism,* in one of its senses, can be understood as a variation on theism. The deist believes in one God, like the theist, but believes that this God cannot or does not involve himself in his creation. *Absolute monism* can be seen as a variation on pantheism or panentheism. The absolute monist holds that God is an absolute unity which is somehow manifested in a less-than-fully-real world of apparent plurality.

The list of views about God also includes views which reject belief in God. *Agnosticism* holds that the truth about God cannot be or is not known and that people should therefore suspend judgment on the question. *Atheism* goes further and actually denies the existence of God. *Naturalism* is a worldview that entails atheism. The naturalist does not believe in any supernatural realm behind nature; she believes that the natural order of things simply exists "on its own." (More will be said about the naturalistic worldview later.) However, while atheism is a belief held by many antireligious people, it is also sometimes held by religious people. The Theravada variety of Buddhism appears to be atheistic, and some atheists have attempted to put forward a humanistic "religion of man" which would not involve a belief in God of any kind.

The Theistic Concept of God

Of all the various views of God, monotheism (henceforth "theism" for short) holds a special importance. It is the dominant view of God in three of the world's great religions: Christianity, Judaism and Islam. Views of God that seem to approximate theism are also found among a significant number of Hindus, and traces or suggestions of such a view can be found in the writings of some of the great philosophers of ancient Greece and in many other religions as well. The reasonableness of theism seems, therefore, to be an issue well worth considering. Before attempting this, however, we need to say a little more about what a theistic conception of God involves.

In the Judeo-Christian tradition, there has emerged a reasonably well-defined list of characteristics that are seen as being essential to God. Some of the attributes on the list are more central than others, and a person rejecting one or more of them might still be recognized as holding to theism or a variation on it. But there is a good deal of agreement about what God—if he exists—is like. Whatever else he may be, God is conceived as a being worthy of worship, the supreme object of religious devotion. This requirement seems to have played a key role in the refinement of the theistic concept of God.

It seems to be a minimal requirement for a being worthy of absolute devotion and worship that he be greater than any other being. No other being exceeds God in power, knowledge or goodness. But theism makes a stronger claim, holding not only that God is greater than any other being as a matter of fact, but that it is impossible for there to be a being greater than God. God's power, knowledge and goodness are therefore seen not merely as being very great but rather as being maximal. God is *omnipotent;* he possesses all the power that a being can possibly have. God is *omniscient;* he knows everything that is possible for a being to know. God is *morally perfect;* his goodness is unsurpassable.

Another way of expressing God's greatness is to say that he is infinite or unlimited. These terms, however, must be understood in a qualified sense. To say that God is infinite in power does not mean that he literally can do anything. It has usually been held, for example, that God cannot create a square circle or bring it about that 2 + 2 = 5; many (though not all) theists would add that he cannot create a person with a morally free will who is determined always to choose what is morally right. The reason for this is not that God lacks some power or ability he might have had, but that these conceptions are logically contradictory and therefore impossible or even meaningless. God's power is the power to bring about anything that is logically possible. In addition, most theists hold that there are certain things God cannot do because of his nature. Being morally perfect, he cannot commit an act of senseless cruelty, for example. God's omnipotence must then be understood as the power to do whatever is logically possible and consistent with God's own essential characteristics. Similar restrictions may have to be placed on the concept of omniscience.

Even with these qualifications, God's power is still infinite in the sense of being unlimited by anything outside himself. God is in no way limited by or dependent on any other being. For this reason God is often described as a *necessary* being. God does not just happen to exist. Since God does not depend for his existence on anything else, and since nothing can threaten his existence, his nonexistence is not really possible. Theists have understood this necessity in two different ways. Some have held that God's existence is logically necessary. On this view, "God does not exist" is thought to express an impossible state of affairs, even if it might seem to be a conceivable one. Others have held that God's necessity is simply grounded in his power and independence. Nothing can in fact threaten God's existence, so his existence is "factually necessary," even if his nonexistence is broadly logically possible. Another way of putting this is to say that God is *self-existent,* meaning literally that his existence depends on nothing outside himself.

Sometimes the medieval term *aseity* is used to denote this characteristic of self-existence.

Since God is a necessary being, he is not "just another being." But he is a being in *some* sense on the traditional theistic account; not only that, but he is a being of a certain type, with a particular nature. God is not just "being-itself," as some philosophers have alleged; such descriptions fail to do justice to the *personal* character of God. That God is personal is implicit in what has already been said, because only a personal being can have power, knowledge and moral perfection. To have power is to be able to do things, to act in certain ways. To know things, a being must be intelligent, have a mind. To be morally perfect is to be perfect in deeds, intentions and thoughts. Although God certainly surpasses human persons in many respects, and some theists insist that God is more than personal, it is clear that God cannot be less than personal. (And it is not even clear what it would be like for a being to be more than personal.) We can put the point cautiously by saying that, of all the things humans have experienced in creation, God most resembles a person.

Since God is personal, it is appropriate to understand him as *acting*. God's primary action is usually understood as that of creation. That God is the Creator means not only, or even primarily, that whatever had a beginning was begun by God, but that whatever exists at any moment exists because of God's will and creative, sustaining power. Everything that exists, other than God, depends on God for its existence, a relationship that is properly stated by describing God as Creator and all other things as creations. (The term "creature" is often used to refer, more specifically, to those parts of the creation that are conscious.)

As Creator, God is therefore continuously active in his creation. (The denial of this is a move in the direction of deism.) This is not to deny a certain autonomy and integrity to the created order, but it does imply that whatever occurs does so because God wills it or permits it to occur. God is everywhere present within his creation in the sense that he can and does bring about some events immediately, and that he knows what occurs everywhere in the same immediate manner. Therefore, it is a mistake to think of God as limited to one region of space. He is properly thought of as *omnipresent,* present everywhere by virtue of his activity and knowledge. Theists have traditionally agreed that this implies that God has no body; he is a *spirit.*

Just as God is not limited by space, so he is, in some way or other, not limited by time. God is an *eternal* spirit. There are some important differences in the way theists have understood God's being eternal. Many have thought of eternity as *timelessness.* On this view, God is thought of as having no temporal succession—no "before and after"—in his existence; he is outside of time altogether. Others have understood divine eternality to mean that God is *everlasting.* On this view, God is, like us, "in time"—in philosophical jargon, he is "temporally located"—but, unlike us, his existence is without beginning or end. In short, God has always existed, and he always will exist. (Note the temporal connotation of these phrases; if they are true of God, he is not outside of time.) He still is not limited by time in the sense that (1) it takes him no time to carry out his actions, (2) his plans and purposes cannot be dimmed or frustrated by the passage of time, and (3) he never desires to change the past. This divergence of views about the nature of God's eternality is not a recent development but goes back hundreds of years. However, in the twentieth century the discussion came to the forefront as a result of the development of *process theologies,* which emphasize the temporal aspect of God's consciousness.

The divergence of views about God's eternality is also reflected in differing views about the degree to which God does not change. Obviously, a perfect being must possess a degree of stability; a being of fickle character would be unworthy of worship. But some classical theists who think of God as timelessly eternal hold to a stronger view: that God is absolutely unchangeable, or *immutable.* On this view, change of any kind is incompatible with perfection. Other theists have understood divine immutability as referring, less radically, to God's character and purposes. These never change, though God is capable of modifying his responses and actions in light of his awareness of what is presently going on in his creation.

This, then, is a brief recounting of the theistic concept of God. God is an eternal, self-existent spirit, unchangeable at least in his basic character and purposes, who exists necessarily. He is a personal being who is omnipotent, omniscient and morally perfect. He is the Creator of all things other than himself, and he is omnipresent in his creation, though without a body.

In recent years, philosophers have done a good deal of interesting work developing and refining these concepts.[1] One of the central problems addressed in this discussion is whether all of the traditional attributes can be applied to God consistently. Atheists often allege that theism can be disproved by taking some attribute of God and demonstrating that, either individually or in combination with other attributes, some absurdity results when the implications of this attribute are worked out to their logical conclusions. If the concept of God is incoherent, then no being could possibly exemplify this concept, in which case theism is false.[2] A similar strategy tries to show that some divine attributes are in conflict with other basic theological doctrines—doctrines about human nature, for example, or God's relation to human beings. The limits of this book do not allow us to explore each of these various debates. However, in the following section, we will look briefly at one of the debates, which has received much attention recently, in order to get a feel for the character and significance of these kinds of discussions.

A Case Study: Divine Foreknowledge and Human Freedom

Arguments that purport to demonstrate some internal tension in the doctrines of orthodox theism are often of great interest to reflective theists, because even if they fail to prove that theism is incoherent, as atheists hope, they are useful in helping theists sort through their theological commitments. Oftentimes, a debate demonstrates the need for some development or nuance of one's views. Various solutions to the problem are proposed, each having important implications for one's broader theology (some implications desirable and others not), and thus one must make a careful "cost analysis" in choosing which to accept. Such is the case with the debate over the relation of divine foreknowledge and human freedom.

The doctrine of divine omniscience is typically taken to imply that God has *foreknowledge*, that is, knowledge of future events. Few would deny that God has knowledge of *some* future events, of course—he obviously knows (we hope!) that the sun will rise tomorrow. More generally, it is uncontroversial that God's knowledge extends to any future event that is causally determined to occur. What is disputed is whether God possesses knowledge of the free choices that humans (and any other free creatures there might be) will make in the future. It is often alleged that if he did, such knowledge would undermine the very freedom of those choices. Consequently, divine foreknowledge and human freedom are incompatible.

Why is it thought that freedom would be undermined by God's knowing in advance the choice that someone will make? A common way of reasoning about the matter is this: Suppose God knows now that Smith will make a phone call to his wife tomorrow at noon. It is a requirement of freedom that one possess *alternate possibilities:* in order for Smith to act freely, it must be that there is more than one thing that he can do. Thus, if Smith is to be free in calling his wife tomorrow at noon, it must be within his power *not* to call his wife at noon. But if God *knows* that Smith will call his wife, then—given that God's knowledge is *infallible*—there really is only one thing that Smith can possibly do at noon tomorrow: call his wife. Since it is not really within Smith's power *not* to call, he does not act freely when he calls. And the same goes for every supposedly free choice that anyone ever makes: if God foreknew it, then it was not really free after all; rather, it occurred of necessity.

As it turns out, this line of reasoning is flawed, though the fallacy it commits is subtle. The mistake lies in thinking that God's knowing that Smith will call his wife tomorrow at noon implies that it is *necessary* that Smith will call (that is, impossible that he will not call) at that time. There is a crucial difference between these two propositions:

(1) Necessarily, if God knows that Smith will call, then Smith will call.

(2) If God knows that Smith will call, then necessarily Smith will call.

Proposition (1) is true, because truth is a conceptual requirement of knowledge (it is impossible for anyone to *know*—as opposed to merely believe—anything that is false). But (1) is not strong enough to make the argument go through; the argument requires (2). The problem with (2), however, is that, if we think about it carefully, we find that there is no good reason to accept it. It does not follow from (1), and it seems prima facie implausible that mere knowledge of an event could cause or otherwise necessitate the event to occur. The argument, convincing as it might initially sound, is flawed.

Unfortunately, the debate is not put to rest as easily as this. It turns out that there is a related argument for the incompatibility of divine foreknowledge and human freedom that, while a bit more complicated, is much more difficult to refute. Suppose that God has known, for all eternity past, that Smith will make a phone call to his wife tomorrow at noon. Again, it is a requirement of freedom that one possess alternate possibilities. Thus, if Smith is to be free in calling his wife tomorrow at noon, it must be within his power *not* to call his wife at noon. And yet, it appears that this is not really within Smith's power. Come noon tomorrow, were Smith *not* to make the call, one of two things would then happen. Either Smith would thereby, at that moment, falsify the belief that God has held about him for all eternity past concerning what he (Smith) would do at this time, or Smith would thereby, at that moment, change the past concerning what God has always believed about him (i.e., Smith would bring it about that God has, for eternity past, always believed that Smith would *not* make the call at that time). But both of these are impossible: God's foreknowledge is infallible—it cannot possibly be mistaken—so there is no chance that Smith will falsify God's past beliefs about him when he acts tomorrow, and it is equally impossible that Smith—or anyone else—can change the past. Even contingent events, *once they have occurred*, take on a kind of necessity: that is, if something occurred in the past, then it is *now necessary* that it occurred. No one, for example, can now change the fact that Kennedy was assassinated on November 22, 1963, even though there was (presumably) something that someone could have done (or not done) that day such that the assassination would not have occurred. It seems clear, then, that there is only one thing that Smith can do tomorrow at noon. And the same goes for every supposedly free choice that anyone ever makes: if God foreknew it, then it was not really free after all; rather, it occurred of necessity.[3]

We are now in a position to see why this problem is of such importance to reflective theists. On the one hand, it is a basic part of orthodox theism that God is omniscient, and omniscience seems to imply foreknowledge. But it is equally a part of orthodoxy that God is just, and that he holds human beings accountable for their actions. It is just for God to do so only if we really are responsible for our actions. But it seems clear that we are responsible only for those actions that we perform freely. (Consider the way that we would excuse a sudden outburst of obscenities from someone with Tourette's syndrome, but not excuse an equivalent outburst from someone who was simply annoyed with those around her.) If divine foreknowledge undermines human freedom, then it seems to follow that God is unjust in holding us responsible for our actions. In this way, the argument from foreknowledge seems to demonstrate an incompatibility among two of God's essential attributes: his omniscience and his justice.

Debates of this kind have been the impetus for important historical theological developments, as well as for revisions to many individuals' personal religious views. There is much at stake here, as different proposed solutions each have significant implications for the broader theology in which it fits. To see that this is so, we will now explore some of the most popular responses to the problem of foreknowledge and freedom. In the interest of space, we will confine our discussion to the Boethian, the theological compatibilist, the Molinist and the open theist solutions, though this list is not exhaustive.[4]

One popular way of trying to resolve the problem of foreknowledge and freedom is by appealing to divine eternality. The sixth-century Christian philosopher Boethius was an important early proponent of the view that divine eternality should be understood as timelessness. Applying this to the foreknowledge problem, Boethius concluded that, since God is "outside of time," God does not, strictly speaking, *fore*know anything. Instead, every moment within creation is *immediately* present to God. Thus, God's means of knowing what we will do in the future is the same as his means of knowing what we are doing now: he simply *observes* it. Since this kind of action is passive (observing something does not itself *actively bring about* that which is observed), there is no reason to think that God's knowledge of what we will do at future times renders those actions necessary, causally determined or otherwise not free.[5]

The difficulty for the Boethian solution, however, is the untoward implications it seems to have for divine sovereignty.[6] In order for the solution to work, it must be, as noted, that God's knowledge of creaturely free choices is passive. But if this is so, then it appears that divine creation involved an enormous limitation of God's sovereignty. Prior to creation, there was no way for God's choice concerning how to create the world to be guided by his knowledge of what the free creatures that he might create would do. Note that, if God is outside of time, there is no literal time before which God knows what creatures will do; there is, in fact, no time before creation. But God's knowledge of creaturely free choices is still *logically subsequent* to his creation: he knows what creatures will do *because* they do it, and not vice versa. Thus, God's knowledge of creaturely choices could not have guided his choice about how to create, on the Boethian view. The implication is that God could not, in creating free creatures, guarantee that things would turn out all right; there was no way that he could *ensure* that his purposes in creation would be fulfilled. Most orthodox theists, however, would consider this consequence unacceptable, regarding it as incompatible with the orthodox doctrine of divine sovereignty. It seems, then, that even if God is in fact outside of time, something else in the divine nature must be operative to successfully reconcile foreknowledge with human freedom.

Theological compatibilists—many of whom also believe that God is outside of time—hold that God knows the future *because he wills it:* that is, he wills *all* of it, including the free choices that each and every person will make.[7] According to the theological compatibilist, everything that occurs in the world occurs because God brings it about. God knows the future exhaustively because, quite simply, he knows the events that he intends to bring about in the future, and his intentions never change. Nevertheless, compatibilists claim, humans are still free. They are free because freedom is compatible with divine determination (being determined by God to do something). The compatibilist arguments for this are more complex than we can go into here, but the upshot is this: the solution involves denying the *principle of alternate possibilities*—which claims that freedom requires being able to do otherwise—and holding, instead, that an agent can be morally free even when there is only one action that is within the agent's power to perform. The compatibilist typically holds that an action is free if the act is one that the agent is not compelled or forced to do, but rather is one that the agent does because she *wants* to do it. In short, a free act is one that expresses the agent's own desires. The compatibilist says that alternate possibilities are required only in the sense that there are other acts the agent could have performed *if* the agent's desires had been different. However, given the agent's actual desires, there was only one action that was truly within the agent's power to perform.[8]

It should be obvious that this kind of move has significant philosophical and theological ramifications. Putting aside the fact that many people (called *incompatibilists*) find the principle of alternate possibilities to be intuitively obvious—that is, putting aside the fact that many take it to express a conceptual requirement of freedom—the theological compatibilist solution seems to face a serious problem in accounting for the existence of evil in the world. Some compatibilists try to draw a distinction between what God "efficaciously causes" and what he "willingly permits," but it is hard to see how the distinction can be sustained, given compatibilist assumptions.[9] Compatibilists are better served to simply bite the bullet and insist that God is the efficacious cause of every event, but then go on to try to argue that a person's action on some occasion can be evil, whereas God's causing the person to perform that action can be good. This happens whenever God causes the individual to perform some action because he sees that the individual's doing so somehow serves some greater good, whereas the individual performs the action out of selfish or otherwise sinful motives. Ultimately, God's will is directed toward bringing about the best possible world, so his actions are perfectly praiseworthy, even when they include causing some human being to sin.

This view, however, appears to run into grave problems when combined with the traditional doctrine of hell, according to which some people are consigned to a place of eternal suffering that will never result in any greater good for those persons. The implication, for the compatibilist, seems to be that God *sacrifices* some people for the sake of bringing about the best possible world. If this is true, then God does not behave lovingly toward everyone but rather only toward those select persons lucky enough to be among "the elect"—those chosen (apparently arbitrarily) to enjoy salvation and, ultimately, eternal communion with God in heaven. Those who take at face value the biblical teaching that "God so loved *the world*" find this implication of compatibilism too high a theological price to pay. (We will return to the problem of hell later, in chapter six.)

A more promising solution, perhaps, developed by Luis de Molina in the sixteenth century, attributes to God *middle knowledge:* knowledge of what any possible free creature would *freely* do in any possible circumstance in which God could place that creature. According to the Molinist solution, God possessed this knowledge prior to creation, and he used this knowledge to decide how he would create the world—that is, which creatures he would create, and which circumstances he would place each of them in. God selected the combination of free creatures and circumstances that he "saw" would result in every creature's freely choosing in such a way that God's ultimate purposes for creation would be fulfilled. At no point was it necessary (nor will it ever be necessary) for God to *cause* anyone to do anything. In this way, God remains sovereign while allowing his creatures freedom in a robust (that is, incompatibilist) sense.

Strictly speaking, the Molinist solution is a solution to the problem of divine sovereignty and human freedom—it explains how God can leave creatures free with respect to their choices while still remaining in complete control of the world—but it straightforwardly implies a solution to the problem of foreknowledge, as well. Since God "saw" how every possible way that he could create the world (every *possible world*, in philosophical parlance) would unfold, and since he is fully aware of which possible world he has in fact chosen to actualize, he knows exactly how the actual world will unfold—including every future free choice that will be made by each creature. Unlike the Boethian solution, then, the Molinist solution, if successful, reconciles divine foreknowledge and human freedom without undermining divine sovereignty.[10]

The primary objection to the Molinist solution, however, is aimed directly at its linchpin: the doctrine of middle knowledge. Critics argue that middle knowledge is *impossible*, and thus even God cannot possess it, because the propositions that God is supposed to know could not possibly be true. The arguments here are complex, but the basic idea is that, prior to creation, there is nothing in existence that could ground the truth value of propositions about what merely possible free creatures would *in fact* freely choose in various, merely possible circumstances. Precisely what it is for an action to be incompatibilistically free is for the action to be determined *by the agent.* So there can be no fact of the matter about what a free creature will do in some situation prior to when the creature is in fact in that situation, making the choice. Prior to creation, then, there was nothing for God to "see" that he could have used to guide his decision about how to create. Middle knowledge, according to its critics, is knowledge of facts that do not exist—which is to say, there can be no such knowledge, even for God.[11]

A fourth solution—one that lacks the support of tradition enjoyed by the other three, but which has received much attention in the contemporary discussion—is that defended by *open theists.* The open theism view simply denies that God's foreknowledge extends to future free choices. Open theists agree with critics of middle knowledge that there can be no knowledge of what merely possible (that is, not-yet-created) free creatures will do, and they extend this to presently existing, free creatures: with regard to their future choices, there is, at present, simply nothing to know. Free creatures share a (perhaps small, but significant) part in creation: their choices are helping to shape the kind of world whose history is progressively being determined. (Thus the meaning of the term "open theism": the cornerstone of the view is that the future is, in part at least, open, in the sense of not-yet-determined.) Thus, open theists insist that God is indeed omniscient—he knows everything that is possible for any being to know—despite his lacking knowledge of the future free choices of his creatures. He knows, for example, what a person is *likely* to do in any given situation, based on his exhaustive knowledge of the person's history and upbringing, present beliefs and desires, character-thus-far-formed, and so on. But with regard to what a free creature *will in fact do* in some scenario that has not yet transpired, there is not yet anything to know, so God's lacking such knowledge does not discount his being omniscient.[12]

Critics of open theism point out that, besides being outside the orthodox mainstream and at odds with tradition, open theism paints a picture in which God takes an enormous risk in choosing to create the world with free creatures in it. If God does not know what any of us will freely choose to do at any given time, then how can he be in control of the world? It seems that God either must be continually scrambling to react to our choices, in such a way as to somehow bring about his good purposes out of the mess that we have made (and are continually making) of things, or he must simply resolve himself to let human history go wherever we take it and thereby risk his purposes for creation being finally thwarted. In the judgment of many believers, either view is incompatible with the doctrine of divine sovereignty that is so central a part of orthodox Christianity. The open theist solution, according to these believers, really does not reconcile divine foreknowledge and human freedom at all: it simply abandons the former—and undermines divine sovereignty in the process, as well.

It is time to take stock. We have seen that there is no easy solution to the problem of foreknowledge and freedom, and whichever solution one adopts will have significant repercussions for one's broader theology. Nevertheless, it does not seem that we have found, in this problem, evidence that theism is false, much less logically incoherent, as some atheists allege. There is a price to be paid for each solution—one must be willing to accept the doctrine of middle knowledge to be a Molinist, for example, or a "risky" view of creation to be an open theist, perhaps—but this is by no means equivalent to having to embrace an obvious logical contradiction, which certainly would be irrational. Reflecting on the nature of human freedom and moral responsibility may require one to carefully revise, refine or qualify other views that one holds—especially concerning such doctrines as divine foreknowledge, sovereignty and creation—but there is no apparent reason that it should lead one to abandon any of these doctrines, much less to abandon theism altogether.

So far as we have seen, then, it still appears reasonable to affirm that theism is logically coherent. And more generally, although it is clear that many concepts used to characterize God must be carefully defined and qualified, no one has convincingly shown, with any such discussion of the divine attributes, that theism, as an overall view, is inconsistent. It is not necessary that a system of beliefs which has been accepted by millions of people for centuries is true, but it would seem reasonable to claim that the burden of proof rests on anyone who asserts that such a system is self-contradictory. No one has been able to show that theism is self-contradictory.

The Problem of Religious Language

In the twentieth century a different type of challenge arose for religious believers. This new challenge was directed not against the logical coherence of theistic concepts, but, even more radically, against the very meaningfulness of belief in God. The objection is that statements like "God exists" or "God loves human beings" are cognitively meaningless; they lack any clear sense. According to proponents of this objection, it is not that we lack evidence that God exists, but that we do not even know what it means to say that God exists. This is the so-called problem of religious language.

The charge that religious beliefs are cognitively meaningless was first made by philosophers known as *logical positivists.* Although logical positivism originated with a group of philosophers in Vienna, who after World War I formed the "Vienna Circle," it became known to English-speaking readers mainly through A. J. Ayer's *Language, Truth and Logic*, first published in 1936 and still in print.

The heart of logical positivism, and the basis of its attacks on the meaningfulness of religious belief, was the *verifiability theory of meaning.* This theory was an attempt to specify the conditions under which a proposition is meaningful. According to this theory, there are two types of meaningful statements. "Analytic" propositions are those statements whose truth or falsehood is determined by the meanings of the words in the statement. According to the positivists, these would include definitions and the truths of mathematics and logic. All nonanalytic meaningful statements are "synthetic." All synthetic propositions must be empirically verifiable: that is, verifiable by what we can experience with our senses.

On the positivist view, analytic statements are solely about language and thus do not give us any information about extralinguistic realities. To give information about reality, or "matters of fact," a proposition must be synthetic and therefore must be empirically verifiable. Since many theological statements purport to give information about God, who is supposed to be more than a linguistic reality, these statements must be empirically verifiable to be meaningful. The positivists claimed that theological assertions were not verifiable and that such statements were therefore cognitively meaningless.

According to Ayer, the positivist view rules out not only theism, but also atheism and agnosticism; after all, if "God exists" is meaningless, it can be neither affirmed nor denied, nor even proposed as a possibility whose truth is not ascertainable.[13] However, in a more extended sense, positivism certainly leads to atheism, if by an atheist we mean someone who declares it is unreasonable to believe in God or even to consider belief as a serious possibility.

Although logical positivism was popular for a period in Anglo-American philosophy, and although some of its characteristic themes continue to surface in other forms (as we shall see), it has not survived as a philosophical movement in its original form. Several powerful objections have been raised against the verifiability theory of meaning.

First, it is not clear that the verifiability theory passes its own test for being a meaningful statement. The theory certainly does not seem to be empirically verifiable, so its proponents must take it as an analytic statement, a statement about the meaning of "meaning." However, most people do not use "meaning" in the way positivists wish to, so as a dictionary definition, the theory is probably false. The only option for the positivist is to propose his theory as a reform, a new stipulation as to the meaning of "meaning." But why should the theist accept this new proposal, given its devastating consequences for religious belief?

Other problems beset the verifiability theory which may be even more serious. Foremost among these is clarifying the notion of verification. Positivism is a form of empiricism, the philosophy that wishes to ground all knowledge in experience. The positivist is suspicious of what cannot be directly seen, touched, felt and so on. As originally developed, therefore, the positivists interpreted verification to be *direct* sensory verification.

The claim that all meaningful synthetic statements must be directly verifiable led to problems, however, for many of the entities postulated by the natural sciences are not directly observable. Quarks and black holes are contemporary examples. Yet logical positivists did not wish their theory of meaning to imply that scientific assertions about these entities are meaningless. To prevent this from occurring, the theory was weakened to allow that a statement was meaningful if it could be verified indirectly. Furthermore, the positivists admitted that the verification did not have to be conclusive, since general statements such as scientific laws can never be proved to be true by any finite set of observations, and that even this indirect, inconclusive verification had to be possible only in principle. When weakened in these ways, the theory, much to the chagrin of its proponents, turns out to allow that religious statements (and indeed just about all statements) can be cognitively meaningful.

Various attempts were made to tighten up the principle to exclude religious statements, but these tightened versions once more were found to exclude scientific statements, as well. No one, in fact, has been able to state a version of the verifiability theory liberal enough to allow meaning to scientific assertions and at the same time restrictive enough to rule out religious beliefs.[14] Thus, although a few well-known philosophers still maintain that religious beliefs are cognitively meaningless because they are not empirically verifiable, it is hard to see why religious believers should regard such accusations with much concern.[15]

Given that no one has yet proven theism to be either self-contradictory or cognitively meaningless, it seems appropriate now to proceed to examine the reasonableness of theism. After all, if we have good reason to believe that theism is true, we also have good reason to think that it is logically consistent and that its assertions are meaningful. What grounds, then, might we have for believing that the God of theism exists?

Natural Theology

As we have already pointed out, theism is held in common by Christianity, Judaism and Islam. The relation between theism and a particular religion like Christianity is as follows: If Christianity is true, then theism is true. The converse does not hold—that is, the truth of Christianity does not follow from the truth of theism—but if theism is true, Christianity *may be* true, and one might even claim that the probability of Christianity's being true is increased. At the very least, one reason for thinking Christianity to be false is eliminated if theism is true.

Philosophers interested in the reasonableness of a religion like Christianity have therefore often proceeded by first attempting to determine the truth of theism. The idea seems to be that one should first establish the truth of theism and then proceed to determine which, if any, of the theistic religions is true. First, one must determine whether God exists, and then one can go on to ask whether God has revealed himself through special events and people. This attempt to determine the truth of theism without assuming the standpoint of a particular religion we shall term *natural theology*. The natural theologian attempts to see what can be known about God independently of any special religious authority. The potential value of natural theology for religious apologetics is evident, since it will be far easier to argue that some individual or book is a revelation from God if it is antecedently known (or probable) that there is a God.

Although natural theology seems worth pursuing, it is by no means evident that this is the best way of coming to know about God, and it certainly would not appear to be the only way. Religious believers typically come to believe in God as a result of (or in the process of) coming to believe in Christianity or some other theistic religion. (In what follows, we will take Christianity as an example of a theistic religion. The cumbersome phrase "or some other theistic religion" will be omitted, but it is implied, nonetheless.) They may come to believe in God by accepting Jesus as one who reveals God. One does not have to first believe in God and then afterward become a Christian. The two may occur simultaneously, and logically the reasons for thinking that theism is true may be the reasons for thinking that Christianity is true.

It is not evident, then, that the success of natural theology is crucial to religious belief. Many Christian theologians, especially Protestants, actually have been hostile to natural theology. Such hostility sometimes stems from the kind of fideism discussed in chapter one, and, indeed, fideism and the rejection of natural theology often are confusedly rolled together. However, a religious believer could reject natural theology without being a fideist. To avoid fideism it is necessary only for the believer to accept the legitimacy of critical reflection on one's beliefs by analyzing them in light of all the evidence and in comparison with alternative views. It is not required that one abstract the core beliefs (theism) from a total set of religious beliefs (such as Christianity) in a way that treats the core beliefs in isolation or ignores the distinctive beliefs of one's religion.

Actually, the distinction between natural theology and revealed theology is not so easy to make as one might think. The believer who rejects natural theology usually claims to know about God because he has experienced God or because God has revealed himself—either directly or through special people, events or sacred writings, often accompanied by miracles or other special signs. It would seem possible, however, to regard such experiences and revelations, if they occur, as a kind of *evidence* for God's existence. And indeed, many natural theologians have developed arguments for God's existence from miracles or from religious experience. In principle such arguments could be developed without presupposing the truth of any particular religion or religious authority, and they would therefore qualify as natural theology by our definition.

If this reasoning is sound, then it may imply that the concept of natural theology is not all that clear and that no sharp line can be drawn between natural theology and other kinds of theology.

Whether or not this is the case, it still seems that there is an important initial distinction to be drawn between believing in God on the basis of arguments, which take as their starting point general features of nature or human experience, and believing in God on the basis of highly specific experiences or events. Even though the latter kind of evidence can be formulated into arguments, most natural theologians have focused on the former kind of argument. And there is a further, significant difference. The natural theologian who begins from general features of nature usually aims to arrive only at that subset of religious beliefs called theism. The person who believes in God on the basis of a historical revelation accompanied by miracles is much more likely to accept theism only as a part of a more inclusive set of beliefs.

In any case, we shall proceed, in the remainder of this chapter and in the next chapter, to look at natural theology in the traditional sense of arguments for God's existence that appeal to general features of human experience. Then, in chapter four, we shall look at religious experiences and other "particular" means of coming to know about God.

Proofs of God's Existence

One way the project of natural theology has been formulated is in the question of whether God's existence can be *proved*. Many philosophers have developed arguments that purport to be such proofs; many others have attempted to find flaws in these arguments.

Before attempting to explain some of these arguments and evaluate their success as proofs, it is necessary to say something about arguments and how they might be judged successful. Philosophers usually think of an argument as a set of statements or propositions (the premises) which show that another statement (the conclusion) is true or which render it probable that the conclusion is true. Arguments can be either deductive or inductive. A good deductive argument is one in which the premises *entail* the conclusion: this relation holds when it is impossible that the conclusion be false *if* the premises are all true. A good inductive argument is one in which the premises render the conclusion *likely* to be true. The more probable it is that the conclusion is true, given the truth of the premises, the stronger the inductive argument. Most arguments given by philosophers for the existence of God have been deductive arguments, although some important contemporary philosophers have put forward inductive arguments.

It is important to see that there are at least three distinct ways of assessing the value of a particular deductive argument. These three ways give us three questions that can be asked about an argument: Is it valid? Is it sound? Does the argument function as a successful *proof*? We will assess these criteria in order.

"Validity" is a term used by logicians in evaluating the formal structure of an argument. An argument is valid whenever the conclusion must be true if the premises are true. In other words, it is valid just in case the premises *entail* the conclusion. The following is an example of a valid argument.

(1) All people from Georgia always speak with a Southern accent.
(2) C. Stephen Evans is from Georgia.
(3) Therefore, C. Stephen Evans always speaks with a Southern accent.

Although this argument is valid, the conclusion is false, since C. Stephen Evans rarely speaks with a Southern accent. The argument is valid because the conclusion would be true *if* the premises were true. But in this case, premise (1) is false.

An argument is *sound* if it is valid *and* all the premises of the argument are true. If an argument is sound, then its conclusion is true. Presumably, those who want to prove God's existence will want, as a minimum, arguments that are sound.

It is clear, however, that the logical criteria of validity and soundness are not enough to characterize a successful proof of God's existence. There are at least two closely related ways that a sound argument might fail as a successful proof.[16] First, it is possible for an argument to be sound without anyone's knowing it to be sound. This could happen if, for example, an argument contained a premise whose truth value was unknown. Consider the following:

(1) The closest, as-yet-undiscovered planet is orbited by two moons.
(2) Therefore, the closest, as-yet-undiscovered planet is orbited by more than one moon.

Obviously, the argument is valid. And the premise *might* happen to be true. If it *is* true, then by definition the argument is sound (valid with true premises). Nevertheless, no one should find this argument convincing in the least, for the obvious reason that no one is in a position to *know* the first premise to be true. (It is built into the premise that the planet in question is at present unknown.) Likewise, a sound argument for God's existence will not be valuable unless all its premises are—or at least *can be*—known to be true.

This brings us to the second way that a sound argument can fail. Consider the following example:

(1) There are humans.
(2) Either there are no humans or God exists.
(3) Hence, God exists.[17]

This argument is logically valid. Any argument of the form

(1) Either *p* or *q*
(2) Not *p*
(3) Therefore *q*

is valid, and this argument can be reduced to that form. Furthermore, the argument *may* even be sound—it certainly is if God exists—and *some* people might even *know* that it is sound (anyone who knows that God exists can know that this argument is sound). Nevertheless, the argument will *convince* no one. It is not altogether easy to articulate precisely what is wrong with this argument, but intuitively the problem is pretty obvious: the only people who would accept the second premise are those who already accept the argument's conclusion.[18] But to be *persuasive*, the premises must be known to be true on grounds *independent* of the conclusion. Only in this way could the argument ever change someone's mind or add conviction to an already-held opinion; only in this way could it be *rationally convincing* and function as a successful proof. Two lessons then can be drawn from this example: First, an argument will fail to be a convincing proof if it employs premises that are just as controversial as (or more controversial than) its conclusion. Second, an argument will fail as a convincing proof if the premises, even if they are known by *some* people, are not known by the intended audience—the individuals to whom the argument is presented and meant to convince.

We have seen, then, that whether an argument is a successful proof depends not only on whether the argument is logically sound but also on whether, how and by whom the argument is known to be sound. To whom should an argument be rationally convincing if it is to be a successful proof? An argument rationally convincing to even one person would possibly be valuable to that person. If this definition of a proof is adopted, then it seems plausible to claim that God's existence can indeed be proven, for reasons that will emerge in chapter three.

Many philosophers would not be happy with such a definition of a proof, however. They have been troubled by the thought that individuals often are mistaken in their beliefs. If one individual claimed to find an argument for God's existence rationally convincing, but nobody else found that argument rationally convincing, surely it is likely that the individual is mistaken. These philosophers want to claim that a genuine proof should be rationally convincing to everyone, or at least to all sane and rational people who have had opportunity to consider the argument carefully. If we define a proof of God's existence as an argument that is rationally convincing to all sane, rational persons, then, as we shall see, no proofs of God's existence can be given.

This conclusion is neither exciting nor disturbing, however, for anyone who has rejected neutralism. Even if the arguments fail as proofs, they may succeed in other ways and have other functions. Furthermore, the claim that in order to know something one must be able to prove it, in the second sense of "proof," is one that carries an implicit commitment to neutralism, for, in effect, one is being asked to adopt a totally disinterested standpoint, accepting only those truths which all sane, rational people would accept. It seems unlikely (for the reasons given in chapter one) that any interesting religious claims can be known or proved in this manner. Hence, the failure to produce a proof of God's existence does not necessarily mean that no one has any justified beliefs about God. Nor does it rule out the possibility that some people arrive at such beliefs by rationally convincing arguments. We will consider the possibility of this in chapter three, as we examine some specific arguments.

3

Classical Arguments for God's Existence

Many different arguments for God's existence have been put forward. Most of them fall into a relatively small number of groups or families. We shall consider four of the most important classes of arguments: ontological, cosmological, teleological and moral.

It is important to recognize that there is no such thing as *the* cosmological argument or *the* teleological argument, although some philosophers have mistakenly assumed this to be the case. Many different versions of each of these arguments have been proposed, and some differ radically from others in the same category. For this reason alone one should be wary of claims to have given a final refutation of one of these types of arguments. It would be difficult to show that an objection applies to *all forms* of an argument and even more difficult to show that no one will ever invent a version of the argument to which the objection does not apply.

In the following discussion we will consider a variety of the versions possible for each type. It is impossible, obviously, to give a careful review of all the arguments that have been proposed or to list all the objections that have been raised. So in each case, we will, after some general comments about the "family" of argument, consider one or more relatively simple versions of the argument. Then we will consider whether this argument could be rationally convincing to anyone. But, of course, even if the specific argument we consider fails to convince, this does not prove that every argument of that type would fail.

Ontological Arguments

Ontological arguments attempt to show that the very concept or idea of God implies his reality: that is, that one's being able to clearly conceive of God somehow implies that God actually exists. Credit for first formulating this argument is usually given to St. Anselm, eleventh-century archbishop of Canterbury. Various versions of the argument have been defended by such famous philosophers as Descartes and Leibniz. The twentieth century saw a great revival of interest in the argument, with thinkers such as Charles Hartshorne, Norman Malcolm and Alvin Plantinga defending different versions of it.

Anselm's original version is developed in his *Proslogion* in the course of some reflections on "the fool who hath said in his heart, There is no God."[1] Anselm reasons that even to deny God's existence, the fool must understand the idea of God. God must exist at least as an idea in the understanding of the fool. What is the idea of God? To Anselm, God is the greatest possible being, "a being than which none greater can be conceived."

Anselm claims that it is greater or better to exist in reality than merely to exist in the understanding (i.e., as a mere concept in someone's mind). Since God is by definition the greatest possible being, says Anselm, it is impossible for God to exist *only* in the understanding of the fool. For in that case, a being greater than God could easily be conceived: namely, a being that exists both in the understanding *and* in reality. Put into numbered steps, the argument goes something like this:

(1) God is the greatest possible being.

(2) God exists at least in the mind.

(3) A being who exists only in the mind is not as great as a being who exists in reality as well as in the mind.
(4) If God existed only in the mind, he would not be the greatest possible being.
(5) Hence, God must exist in reality as well as in the mind.

As might be expected, this argument has met with many objections, for the claim that the existence of something can be inferred merely from its definition is implausible to most people. Gaunilo, a contemporary of Anselm, produced a parody of the argument which attempted to prove that a perfect island—"an island than which none greater can be conceived"—must exist. Anselm's reply to this was essentially that the concept of God is a unique one. God, unlike islands and other finite objects, is a *necessary* being. The implication is that the concept of a "greatest or most perfect possible island" may not be coherent. Perhaps for any island we conceive, we could always conceive a more perfect one. But only a necessary being can be a greatest possible being. The significance of Anselm's reply will be made evident shortly.

A famous objection made by Immanuel Kant and others is that one cannot legitimately think of "existence" as a property that an entity may or may not have, or may have in varying degrees. To say of something that it exists is not to say that it has some property like "being red," but that the concept of the entity in question, with all its properties, has been actualized. In other words, the concept is exemplified by something in reality. When we think of an object, we always implicitly think of it as existing. But if existence is not a property, then it cannot be a property that adds to God's greatness, which is required by the argument. The debate whether existence is a property (or whether "exists" is a proper predicate) is not one we can resolve here, though it does seem safe to claim that existence is no *ordinary* property.

Another popular objection to Anselm's argument is that it tells us only about the definition of God; it cannot tell us whether anything satisfies that definition. Anselm tells us, quite properly, that when we think of God, we think of him as a real being, even as a necessarily real being, a being who cannot fail to exist. Such a definition, however, like all definitions, only tells us what God would be like if he existed. It cannot establish the fact *that* he exists; it cannot tell us whether the concept of God is *exemplified* in the actual world.

Contemporary versions of the argument have focused on the concept of necessary existence, which Anselm employed in his reply to Gaunilo and in chapter three of his *Proslogion*. Some philosophers, such as Norman Malcolm, have claimed that Anselm actually developed two arguments. The first emphasized existence as a "great-making property," which Malcolm thinks is fallacious, since existence is not a property at all. The second posited the concept of necessary existence.[2] The gist of the second argument, as Malcolm formulates it, is as follows: God is, by definition, a being who does not merely happen to exist. God can neither come into existence nor pass out of existence, since a being who could do either simply would not be God. It follows from this that if God exists at all, then his existence is necessary. If he does not exist, then his existence is impossible. But either God exists or he does not exist, so God's existence is either necessary or impossible. Since it does not seem plausible to say that God's existence is impossible, it follows that his existence is necessary. More formally, the argument can be put like this:

(1) If God exists, his existence is necessary.
(2) If God does not exist, his existence is impossible.
(3) Either God exists or he does not exist.
(4) Therefore, God's existence is either necessary or impossible.
(5) God's existence is possible (not impossible).
(6) Therefore, God's existence is necessary.

How shall we evaluate this argument? Is it formally valid? It certainly appears to be. Is it sound? To be sound, the premises must all be true. Of the premises, the one most doubtful is premise (5).

How do we know that God's existence really is possible? The premise appears innocuous enough; it seems as if we are saying simply that there might be a God. It turns out, however, to be a rather strong claim, since God's existence is possible only if it is necessary. Why should the atheist not reject (5) and claim that, when the matter is fully understood, God's existence can be seen to be impossible? The atheist could argue that since God does not in fact exist, he never has and never will exist, and, moreover, that there is no way the world that includes God's existing at any time could have possibly been.

On the other hand, anyone who believes that God actually exists will have to judge that this premise is true and that the argument is therefore sound. For the possibility of God's existence surely follows from the actuality of his existence. Still, we should recall that a successful proof must be more than merely sound. It must be rationally convincing. Here the argument seems to fail, for it is hard to see why an atheist should not reject premise (5) and steadfastly maintain the impossibility of God's existence. And even though theists will judge the argument sound, it will be rationally convincing to theists only if they can somehow *know* that God's existence is possible *without* inferring it from his actual existence. Recall, from our discussion in chapter two, that for an argument to be rationally convincing, the premises must be known or rationally believed on grounds independent of the conclusion.

Even if the argument fails as a rationally convincing proof, however, it may still accomplish other tasks. Alvin Plantinga, a defender of a contemporary version of the ontological argument, contends that although the argument may not be a proof, it does show that it is reasonable to believe in God. The key premise, that God's existence is possible, although it may not be known, is a proposition that could reasonably be accepted: the argument shows the "rational acceptability" of theism.[3] This seems sound, but it should be noted that the atheist can perhaps make a similar claim: it is not clearly contrary to reason to assert that God's existence is impossible. In fact, all the atheist really needs is the claim that it is *possible* that God does not exist; with this premise, he can modify the argument into an argument for atheism, as follows:

(1) If God exists, his existence is necessary.
(2) It is possible that God does not exist.
(3) Therefore, God's existence is not necessary.
(4) Therefore, God does not exist.

Karl Barth interprets Anselm's argument not as a proof but as an attempt to understand more deeply what is accepted by faith.[4] It does seem very plausible that Anselm's purposes in putting forward this argument may be very different from those of contemporary philosophers who have defended the argument. In any case, regardless of the value of the ontological argument as a proof, reflection on it does deepen our appreciation of God as a necessary being.

The argument also serves the function of "smoking out" the atheist. If the argument is valid, then the person who wishes to deny that God exists must claim that God's existence is impossible. That may be a stronger claim than the person in question initially wished to make. This last point can be generalized into a moral that can be applied to all the theistic arguments. The arguments can be rejected, but the person who rejects them pays a price. For to deny a proposition is logically equivalent to asserting another proposition. To deny *p* is to assert not-*p*. In some cases, the assertions required to reject theistic arguments may be troublesome ones—a point that we will see demonstrated several times in this chapter.

Cosmological Arguments

Cosmological arguments are, as the name implies, attempts to infer the existence of God from the existence of the cosmos or universe. Such arguments may take as their starting point the existence of the universe as a whole, the existence of particular objects or the existence of even one individual object. These arguments are sometimes called *first-cause arguments* because they attempt to infer that God must exist as the first or ultimate cause of the universe.[5]

The historical roots of the cosmological argument go back to the Greek philosophers Plato and Aristotle, but it was more fully developed in the medieval period by Thomas Aquinas and Duns Scotus. Of the five arguments for God's existence given by Aquinas in his *Summa Theologica,* the first three appear to be versions of the cosmological argument. In the early modern period Samuel Clarke and Gottfried Leibniz defended their own versions. In the contemporary discussion the argument has been defended by Richard Taylor and Richard Swinburne, among others.[6] Swinburne defends the argument in a somewhat novel way by treating it as an inductive argument, or probability argument, rather than a strictly deductive argument.

We have already noted a distinction between versions which take as a premise the existence of the universe as a whole and those which take as their starting point the existence of some part of the universe. These we will term *whole arguments* and *part arguments,* respectively. In addition to this, it is important to distinguish between versions of the argument that presuppose that the universe had a beginning in time and those which do not. The former versions we will call *temporal arguments,* while the latter we will call *nontemporal arguments.*

Temporal versions of the argument contend (or assume) that the universe had to have a beginning, a first moment of existence.[7] A cause is necessary to explain its existence in that first moment, and God is inferred to be that cause. In these versions God is the "first cause" in a temporal sense. He is the one who began the series of events we call the universe by bringing into existence the initial objects that composed the universe. By itself, this argument seems to demand only a deistic conception of God, but someone who holds to it can accept theism consistently by claiming also that God continues to be involved in his creation.

That the universe had a beginning in time has been argued in various ways. Some have claimed that an *actual* infinite temporal series, such as the past would be if the universe were eternal, is impossible.[8]

Others have claimed that scientific theories, such as the big bang theory, provide evidence for the universe's having had a beginning.[9]

We shall not pursue these claims further because the majority of philosophers who have defended the cosmological argument have claimed that it is sound regardless of whether the universe had a beginning. Aquinas, Leibniz, Clarke and Taylor have defended nontemporal versions. They have all claimed that God is the necessary cause of the existence of the universe, both now and for as long as the universe has existed, even if it has always existed. God is the reason why there is a universe at all, regardless of whether the universe is young, old or infinitely old.

What is it about the universe that supports the claim that it requires a cause and that its cause must be God? The usual answer hinges on what may be termed the *contingency* of the universe. If we look around us at the universe, each object we see (and all of them, taken collectively) appears to be the kind of thing which does exist but might easily have not existed. There seems to be no natural reason (that is, no reason given in terms of the laws of nature) why the objects of our universe exist or even why there should be a universe at all. In short, we find in the natural order no explanation for why there is something rather than nothing. The things we see do not appear to be things which had to exist, things which exist *necessarily*. Rather, they are all contingent: things which do exist but might not have. It is then natural to wonder why they exist. What is the cause of their existence? If the cause of a thing is something contingent, then the existence of that "something" will also require an explanation. Ultimately, the explanation of any contingent being's existence will be incomplete unless it culminates in the causal activity of a *necessary* being—a being that cannot fail to exist, a being that is the cause of the existence of all contingent beings. A necessary being is the only kind of being whose existence requires no further explanation. In short, there is an ultimate explanation for the existence of a contingent being only if there exists a necessary being. We can formalize the key elements in this argument as follows:

(1) Some contingent beings exist.
(2) If any contingent beings exist, then a necessary being must exist (because contingent beings require a necessary being as their ultimate cause).
(3) Therefore, there exists a necessary being (which is the ultimate cause of the existence of contingent beings).

As many critics have pointed out, this version of the cosmological argument is not a proof of God's existence because, even if it is successful, it proves only the existence of *some* necessary being that is the cause of all contingent beings. (It does not even establish that there is only one such being.) It does not establish that this being is omnipotent, omniscient, perfectly good and so forth—attributes a being must possess to be God. Nevertheless, given that God is taken by theists to be both a necessary being and the Creator of the universe, a successful cosmological argument would obviously constitute a crucial *part* of a cumulative case for theism.

Once more, we have before us an argument that appears to be formally valid, so the interesting questions are whether it is sound and whether it functions as a successful proof. Before attempting to decide these questions, however, we will first deal with three common and popular objections to the argument. These objections may have force against some versions of the argument, but despite their popularity they are irrelevant with respect to the version we are considering. Pointing this out will bring into focus the real issues.

Objection 1. The universe might always have existed. *Reply:* This objection applies only to temporal versions of the argument. Our version does not assume anything about the age of the universe; it is compatible with the possibility that the universe has always existed. The thrust of the argument is that the present existence of contingent objects requires that there be a necessary being.

Objection 2. If everything requires a cause for its existence, then God also requires a cause for his existence. *Reply:* This objection is misguided, because the proposition that everything requires a cause for its existence is not a premise of the argument. There is, in premise (2), an implicit assumption that all *contingent* beings require a cause for their existence, and perhaps even some implicit assumptions about the kind of cause that contingent beings require. But God is not a contingent being. It is not arbitrary to deny that God has a cause, because, if God did have a cause, he would not be God. As we discussed in chapter two, only a self-existent or necessary being can qualify for the title of "God," and it makes no sense to ask about the cause of such a being.

Objection 3. The argument commits the *fallacy of composition*, which occurs whenever one observes that each of the members of some collection has a certain property and infers that the collection, as a whole, must have that same property. For example, it would be a fallacy to infer that one's family as a whole weighs less than two hundred pounds on the grounds that every individual member of the family weighs less than two hundred pounds. Likewise, even though every individual object in the universe has a cause, we cannot infer that the universe as a whole has a cause. The existence of each object in the universe can be explained in terms of other objects, and there is no need to explain the existence of the whole. *Reply:* This objection is irrelevant, since the argument, as we have presented it, is a part argument rather than a whole argument (recall the way these terms were defined earlier). In other words, the version of the argument we are considering references only individual contingent objects, not the collection of all contingent objects.

Furthermore, although many versions of the cosmological argument do begin by claiming that the universe as a whole is contingent and requires a cause, it is by no means obvious that these whole arguments commit a fallacy. Inferences about the composition of a whole from its parts are not always fallacious. One can validly infer from the fact that every state of the United States is in the Northern Hemisphere that the United States, as a whole, is in the Northern Hemisphere. It seems plausible that if every object in the universe is contingent, then the universe as a whole is contingent. The mere fact that there are many contingent objects in the universe certainly does not, by itself, entail that the whole collection is necessary. Regardless, the version of the argument we are considering does not make use of any "part-to-whole" inference, so we can safely put objection (3) aside.

With these three irrelevant objections out of the way, we can now consider the soundness of the argument. This is made considerably easier by the fact that the argument has only two premises.

Premise (1) says simply that some contingent objects exist. This seems highly plausible, but it has not been accepted by everyone. Some people might want to hold that the matter (or energy) in the universe is eternal. Particular objects come and go, but according to the law of conservation of mass-energy, the matter of which they are composed is neither created nor destroyed. So far, this is not a real objection to the argument, which is consistent with the eternality of the matter in the universe. But suppose someone went further and claimed that the matter composing the universe is not only eternal but also necessarily existent: that is, it could not have failed to exist. If this person then went on to claim that the only objects that *really* exist are the eternal constituents of matter (whatever those may be), then he would be denying premise (1). He would be saying that no contingent beings exist.

It is important to see how extreme this conclusion really is. It implies that, strictly speaking, there are no chairs, no human bodies, no planets, no objects of any kind other than the eternal constituents of matter—a claim most would consider self-evidently false. Without this last stipulation (that only eternal objects are real), the objection might seem more plausible, but in this case, it does not strictly undermine the argument, because the objector's view would still imply the existence of a necessary reality as the cause of complex contingent beings. However, in this case, the cause would be matter itself. The eternal constituents of matter would be "necessary beings" and would thus satisfy the requirement of the argument's conclusion. In any case, someone who thinks of matter as "necessary" thereby implies that at least one of the features of the theistic God is actually a feature of the natural world. One might say that it is not so much that God's existence is being denied as that the existence of God *as a person distinct from the universe* is being denied. Implicit in the claim that matter is necessarily existent (or that bits of matter are necessarily existent) is something much like a commitment to pantheism. The person who rejects the argument is committed to saying not merely that the material universe has in fact always existed but that the universe (at least its ultimate parts) could not possibly fail to exist. It appears, then, that rejecting premise (1) comes at a steep price: at best, it commits one to a rival metaphysical perspective that is either pantheistic or close to it.[10]

It seems more likely that contemporary Western critics of the argument would quarrel with premise (2), which states that if any contingent beings exist, then a necessary being must exist, because a contingent being requires as its ultimate cause a necessary being. This assumption is complex and could be denied in two ways. First, someone might claim that in certain cases the existence of a contingent being can be uncaused. Second, someone might claim that although every contingent being requires a cause for its existence, there is an infinite series of contingent beings, each of which has another contingent being (or beings) as its cause. In summary, one can reject premise (2) by claiming either that some contingent beings have no cause or that there is an infinite series of contingent causes.

The first, or "no cause," objection is essentially a claim that some contingent objects have no explanation; they just *exist.* Their existence is what is often called a "brute fact." The defender of the argument will respond that it is unreasonable to claim that the existence of any contingent thing is simply a brute fact. (The defender's reasons for claiming this will be made clear, momentarily.)

The second response—the "infinite-series-of-causes" view—is somewhat different, since the proponent of this objection claims that each and every contingent thing has a cause: namely, some other contingent thing or set of things. Since the series is infinite, no individual lacks a cause. The proponent of the cosmological argument can deal with this infinite-series view in two ways. First, she might concede that each and every individual contingent object has an explanation, but claim that what has not been explained is the existence of the whole series. Why is there an infinite series of contingent objects, rather than nothing at all? This effectively converts the argument from a part argument to a whole argument. This will require the defender of the argument to claim that the contingency of the whole of the universe can validly be inferred from the contingency of all its parts.

The second option for the proponent of the argument is to claim that the explanations of existence offered by the infinite-series view are unsatisfactory, because an infinite series of contingent causes would never provide an *ultimate* explanation for the existence of any contingent being. Contingent object A exists because of contingent object B, but since B's existence is contingent, it is natural to ask why B exists, as well. To the extent that the question is unanswered, one could conclude that A's existence has not been completely explained. This does not mean that the explanation is not complete enough for ordinary, practical purposes, but it does mean that the explanation is in some sense incomplete.

This is why the defender of the cosmological argument finds the infinite-series view defective. To postulate an infinite series as an explanation for the existence of a particular contingent object is really to admit that no final, determinate explanation can be given. In this way, the infinite-series view turns out, at bottom, to share something in common with the no-cause view. Both claim that the existence of contingent beings—either select contingent beings or the entire, infinite series of contingent beings, as a whole—has no determinative cause; both therefore entail that there is, in the final analysis, no complete explanation for the existence of such beings. The proponent of the cosmological argument, on the other hand, accepts some version of what is called the ***principle of sufficient*** *reason.*[11] She holds that there must be a finally adequate explanation, both for the existence of every particular contingent being and for the entire series of contingent beings. The existence of contingent beings—either individually or collectively—cannot be a brute fact, since such beings do not themselves explain their existence.

The person who denies premise (2) of the argument is therefore denying the principle of sufficient reason. He is claiming that (at least some) contingent objects have no ultimate reason for being; they just *exist.* Once more, it is evident that rejection of the argument carries with it a price. The typical motivation for rejecting the cosmological argument is that one prefers a rival metaphysical system: most likely, naturalism, the view that the natural order exists "on its own." The naturalist rejects the argument by claiming that the existence of contingent beings is ultimately just a brute fact. Provisional and partial explanations of why some beings exist can be given in terms of other finite beings, of course, but no final explanation can be given of why there should be such things as finite beings at all. This is the price tag for being a naturalist.

If we ask, Why are there any beings at all? the naturalist will answer either that there is no reason or that the question is a meaningless one which cannot be answered. Some naturalists have taken the latter position.[12] Others, particularly some of the atheistic existentialists, have taken the former line. Writers such as Jean-Paul Sartre and Albert Camus have described the world as *absurd,* meaning that no reason can be given for its existence. The world is the sort of thing which ought to have an explanation, but does not.[13]

Is the cosmological argument rationally convincing? It may be to some people. Many people have had powerful experiences of what may be called the contingency of things in the universe, including their own existence. Although our familiarity with finite objects may indeed breed contempt or at least a lack of wonder about them, most people can recall experiences in which they have suddenly become aware of the enormous oddity that anything exists at all—or the oddity that just *these* particular things exist. We might call these "experiences of cosmic wonder." It may be that one's evaluation of the cosmological argument turns heavily on how such experiences are interpreted and evaluated. If one dismisses the experience as meaningless, trivial or neurotic, one will dismiss the question Why do things exist? as meaningless, trivial or neurotic. If one accepts the experience as significant, then one will admit that the question posed by the cosmological argument is meaningful. One can meaningfully ask, Why is there a universe? Here, the debate will turn on whether humans have a right to expect an answer—whether the universe in some sense *must* make sense. This is, in effect, the question of whether the principle of sufficient reason is true.

There may be no way of *proving* that the question does indeed have a satisfactory answer. (One might, of course, try to show that the consequences of rejecting the principle of sufficient reason in other contexts are unacceptable.) Hence, if by "proof" we mean an argument that is rationally convincing to everyone, the cosmological argument certainly fails. But it does powerfully evoke and articulate the theistic view of the relation that holds between God and contingent beings. The person who finds meaningful the question Why is there anything at all? and who is unwilling to accept that there is no satisfactory answer to the question, may very well find the argument convincing.

Certainly, the argument helps us to better understand the nature of theism and how it differs from rival views. It helps us to see that the question of whether God exists is not a question like Is there a Loch Ness monster? The question about God is not merely a question about another entity but rather a question about the character of the universe as a whole. The rejection of the cosmological argument implicitly carries with it a commitment to a rival metaphysical view, such as pantheism or naturalism. Ultimately, the question is not Can God's existence be proved? but rather Which metaphysical view is most plausible? A theist may find the argument helpful in defending her conviction that theism is indeed a reasonable way of viewing the universe.

It is worth reiterating how limited a conclusion the cosmological argument reaches. By itself, the argument only seems to show the existence of a necessary being that is the cause of the universe. While this does include some key elements of the theistic conception of God, it obviously leaves out quite a few important ones. The conclusion is compatible with many views of God. So, even if it is successful, the cosmological argument hardly constitutes more than an entering wedge into the knowledge of God. If someone accepts the conclusion, the proper attitude for him to adopt is surely a desire to learn more about God. Such a person should show an alert sensitivity about how he may obtain additional knowledge of God.

Teleological Arguments

In a broad sense, a teleological argument is also a cosmological argument: it too begins with the existence of the cosmos. It begins, however, not merely with its existence but with its character as a cosmos, an orderly universe. It is often referred to as *the argument from design.*

Like the cosmological argument, the teleological argument finds its roots in classical Greece. And it is clearly present in medieval times as the fifth of Aquinas's "Five Ways" of proving God's existence. In terms of popularity, however, the heyday of the argument was the eighteenth and early nineteenth centuries. A particularly famous version was developed by William Paley (1743-1805), an English theologian. In the contemporary discussion the argument has been defended by Richard Taylor, F. R. Tennant and Richard Swinburne.[14] Tennant and Swinburne, particularly, have developed the argument not as a strict deductive proof but as an attempt to show the *probability* of theism.

The teleological argument begins from the fact that the natural world appears to exhibit purposive order or design, and infers that its cause must therefore be an intelligent designer.

Aquinas's version of the argument is a good illustration:

> The fifth way is taken from the governance of the world. We see things which lack knowledge, such as natural bodies, act

> for an end, and this is evident from their acting always, or nearly always, in the same way, so as to obtain the best result. Hence it is plain that they achieve their end, not fortuitously, but designedly. Now whatever lacks knowledge cannot move towards an end, unless it be directed by some being endowed with knowledge and intelligence; as the arrow is directed by the archer. Therefore some intelligent being exists by whom all natural things are directed to their end; and this being we call God.[15]

Aquinas here claims that many entities in nature act for an end or *telos.* He does not give any examples, but it is not hard to do so. Most animals, for example, appear to be self-regulating mechanisms, designed to maintain their own existence and reproduce themselves. Many of the parts of the animals contribute to this overall goal by realizing some more particular end or goal. Lungs exchange oxygen for carbon dioxide; hearts pump blood throughout the body.

Aquinas mentions two features present in nature that together imply design. The first is *order.* Things in nature "act always or nearly always in the same way." The second feature is *value.* The order in nature brings about results that are good. We shall term this kind of order *beneficial order.* Clearly, Aquinas thinks that a regular, orderly process which achieves a beneficial result is evidence that one is dealing with intelligent design. Beneficial order, he says, does not occur by chance.

How does Aquinas know this? Why couldn't orderly processes which bring about beneficial results be the product of chance? Contemporary defenders of the argument, such as Taylor and Swinburne, have admitted that it is not logically impossible for these processes to occur by chance. Thus, on their view, the argument fails as a strict deductive proof. However, although it is perhaps possible for such results to occur by chance, it is, they claim, implausible or improbable. Hence, the argument shows the probability or plausibility of theism: that is, theism provides the most likely explanation of the evidence that we observe. This kind of reasoning is often called "inference to the best explanation."[16]

One way (though perhaps not the only way) of defending the crucial claim that it is improbable that beneficial order could be the result of chance is to make an appeal to our experience of analogous entities. Complex machines, like watches and cameras, show the same kind of complex, beneficial order as do natural objects. We know that these machines are the result of intelligent design, and it is reasonable to conclude that objects in nature which are analogous to these machines are probably to be explained in an analogous manner. Paley's famous argument proceeds in this way, and David Hume's *Dialogues Concerning Natural Religion* gives a well-known statement of the argument in the form of an analogy. Hume also presents many criticisms of the argument, some of which will be considered presently.

It is worth noting that teleological arguments, like cosmological arguments, can be divided into those which begin with the whole of nature and those which begin with parts of nature. The former attempts to show that nature as a whole must be understood as one teleological system. The latter takes as its starting point the existence of particular teleological systems within nature. The advantage of the "whole" type of argument is that the conclusion will obviously be the existence of a cause of the whole of nature. The disadvantage is that it is difficult to show that the universe as a whole aims at some end or goal. It may, but it does not seem evident that it does. The "part" type of argument is therefore easier to defend, but if one is not careful, the argument is subject to charges of committing the fallacy of composition, in that it draws an inference about the cause of the whole of nature from observations about the character of some part(s) of nature. The fallacy can be avoided by arguments that reason by way of inference to the best explanation, but, as we will see, concerns may be raised about the likelihood of the conclusion.

Let us now formulate some versions of the teleological argument and consider their merits and demerits. The following is a simple version:

(1) There exist in nature many examples of beneficial order.
(2) Beneficial order is best explained as the result of an intelligent designer.
(3) Therefore, nature is probably the result of an intelligent designer.

The conclusion can at best be probable for two reasons: (1) an inference about the whole of nature is being drawn from an observation about parts of nature; (2) it is not certain that beneficial order can only come from intelligence.

Most criticisms of this argument will focus on premise (2). Must we explain the existence of beneficial order in nature as the work of a designer? Alternative formulations of the argument shift the criticism elsewhere. For example, the argument could be put as follows:

(1) Nature contains many instances of design.
(2) Designed entities are the result of a designer.
(3) Therefore, nature is probably the work of a designer.

This formulation makes the second premise virtually tautologous, but now the critic will question the truth of the first premise. Is the appearance of design in nature *genuine* design, or is it *merely apparent*? If the first premise is read as "Nature contains many instances of apparent design," then its truth seems undeniable, but then the argument will not be valid. The conclusion—that nature is the work of a designer—is not even rendered likely by the premises. The underlying problem remains how one knows that the beneficial order that we find in nature is not simply, in Aquinas's words, "fortuitous."

The analogical versions of the argument, as mentioned, try to confront this problem head-on. For example, we might argue as follows:

(1) Objects in nature are analogous to manmade machines, in that their parts work together to achieve some end or purpose.
(2) Manmade machines are the result of intelligent design.
(3) Analogous effects tend to have analogous causes.
(4) Therefore, objects in nature are probably the result of something analogous to intelligent design.

As we see from this, the appeal to analogy can generate a self-contained argument. Alternatively, the considerations appealed to here could be employed to back up the debatable second premise in our original argument.

In general, criticisms of teleological arguments can be divided into two groups. The first includes those criticisms which attack the strengths of the argument by claiming that intelligent design is unnecessary to explain the order in the universe. The second group of criticisms focuses on the religious worth of the argument, questioning whether the intelligent designer that the argument infers is identical to the God of theism. Both kinds of criticisms are given classical statements in Hume's *Dialogues Concerning Natural Religion.*

Let us take the former type of attack first. Hume considers the argument mainly in its analogical form; hence, many of his criticisms center on the strength of the analogy between the natural order and human machines. He objects, for one, that the universe is too singular a phenomenon to form hypotheses about its cause.[17] Since we have no experience of universe making, we have no way of testing alternative hypotheses about its cause. However, if Hume were right here, then *no* argument from analogy would have any value, for Hume is in effect claiming that we cannot trust an analogy unless we have repeated direct experiences of what we are making an analogical inference about: in this case, universes. But if we *had* such direct experience, analogous reasoning would be unnecessary.

A more serious objection, however, is Hume's claim that alternative explanations of the order of the universe are possible. Perhaps the order in the universe is somehow inherent in matter.[18] Perhaps the order of the universe is, in reality, the result of blind, mechanical processes.[19] Though Hume preceded Darwin, we get a sense of the full force of Hume's objection when we consider it in light of Darwin's theory of evolution. Interpreted naturalistically, Darwinian evolution gives an explanation of the order of the universe that is a rival to theistic explanations. On the Darwinian account, facts about order in nature—for example, that creatures are so well adapted to their environments or that the organs of creatures are mutually coordinated—are explained by random variations and the principle of "survival of the fittest." Without delving into details, the basic idea is this: A certain amount of random variation occurs in nature. (In contemporary terms, one common way this variation comes about is through the genetic recombination that occurs when organisms that reproduce sexually pass on their genetic material to their offspring.) When a variation occurs that gives a creature some edge over its competitors, it will be more likely to survive to reproductive age and thus be able to pass on to its offspring the favorable change (encoded in its genetic makeup). Given enough time, what appears to be design can be explained mechanistically. Clearly, it is the popularity of evolutionary theory, more than anything else, which has eroded the credibility of the traditional teleological argument.

To this evolutionary challenge, three lines of response are possible. First, some have directly attacked the theory of evolution itself, arguing that a kind of divine creation "from scratch" provides a superior scientific explanation. This is the position of some who have advocated the teaching of "creation science" as an alternative to evolution.

A second line of response is to concede that an evolutionary process has occurred, but to argue that the process is not one that can be understood or explained purely mechanistically. Chance variation and natural selection are inadequate to explain the order which has evolved. Instead, it seems more plausible to see the process as one guided, at least at certain points, by intelligent design.

A third response concedes the validity of Darwinian or neo-Darwinian theories as *scientific* explanations of the order in the universe, but questions whether an *ultimate* explanation is not still required. Mechanical explanations and teleological/design explanations are not always incompatible. If a person who desires to achieve some result—say, the production of shoes—designs a machine to achieve that result, then two kinds of explanations are possible. One can explain the appearance of the shoes mechanically, in terms of the operation of the machine. But, of course, the machine operates as it does *because* it is a means for achieving the result; it was designed to do so. Hence, a more complete explanation of the result in terms of the purpose of the machine's designer is also legitimate. It is not by accident that the machine achieves its beneficial results.

In a similar way the defender of the teleological argument might claim that the evolutionary process, even if it is a mechanical process, is simply the means whereby God, the intelligent designer, realizes his purposes. The evolutionary process, if it does indeed occur, occurs only because the laws of nature operate as they do. These laws are themselves a clear example of order whose ultimate outcome is beneficial order. The defender of the teleological argument can therefore claim that evolution in no way lessens the beneficial order of the universe or the need to explain that order. Rather, evolution simply increases our understanding of the complex and ingenious means whereby the designer God realizes his purposes.

In evaluating this third kind of response, the question we must ask is whether the basic order of the universe—the natural laws which have operated to bring about the apparent design in nature (if evolution is true)—is a brute fact. It seems clear that the laws of nature and physical constants (e.g., the mass of an electron, the speed of light, Planck's constant, etc.) are contingent; they could have been different. Why, then, do we have the laws that we do? The critic of the argument seems forced to claim that no explanation can be given. But to the defender of the argument, it seems arbitrary and implausible to say that such laws are simply brute facts.

Recent developments in theoretical physics seem to substantiate the defender's incredulity. Physicists are now able to calculate what the universe would have been like, in certain respects, had one or more of these laws or physical constants been different. What they tell us is that, had certain values been even minutely different, the emergence of life—by evolutionary or any other conceivable natural means—would have been impossible. In fact, the odds of a single universe *just happening* to have a combination of such values that makes the emergence of life possible are *infinitesimally* small. For this reason, it seems to many that the universe has been "fine-tuned": that is, intentionally designed for the (eventual) emergence of living beings like ourselves. *Fine-tuning arguments* have reinvigorated discussion of the argument from design, once regarded by many to have been decisively put to rest by the Darwinian theory of evolution.

Critics of the "new" design argument are not without reply, however. Some point out that while the probability of a *single* universe just happening to have the "right" values for life is indeed very small, if there are very many actual universes—perhaps infinitely many—each with different laws of nature and physical constants, then it was all but inevitable that at least one would have the "right" combination that allows life to emerge in it. (That universe, of course, is our own.) There are several ways this possibility might obtain: Perhaps the history of the universe is an eternal cycle of one big bang followed (eventually) by a big crunch, followed, in turn, by another big bang and so on, ad infinitum, with each big bang randomly generating a different set of laws and physical constants for the subsequent universe. Or perhaps our universe is but one of an infinite number of causally and spatiotemporally isolated universes, each with its own, unique set of laws and physical constants. So long as these possibilities cannot be ruled out, the design argument remains inconclusive.[20]

To say that it is inconclusive, however, is not to say that it is without rationally persuasive force. Once again, the argument from design—like any good theistic argument—demonstrates that there is a price to be paid in rejecting its conclusion. The price that an atheist seems forced to pay, in this case, is this: she must claim that there is *in fact*, in one form or another, an infinite number of actual universes, each with different physical laws and constants. In addition to being a seemingly wild claim, the problem with this view is that it is, at present at least, highly speculative and unsubstantiated by empirical evidence. This is a serious problem for a naturalist, who typically prides herself in holding to a thoroughly scientific worldview. The naturalist is forced to make a claim about the physical world that receives no empirical support and is, instead, motivated by ideological reasons (in particular, the desire to retain her naturalism). In this way the teleological argument pushes the naturalist to make a "profession of faith" that belies her ostensive commitment to science. This seems a high price to pay, indeed.

Furthermore, the fine-tuning argument would likely retain much of its force even if there *were* substantial empirical evidence to support the many-universe theory. This is so because on the most plausible versions of the theory, there is (or was) some process that generates multiple universes. But on this view it would have to be the case that the conditions were just right for the "many-universe generator" to be able to "work." But why, we should ask, were these favorable conditions in place, given that there could have been other, unfavorable conditions in place, instead (in which case there would not have been many universes)? The explanatory need for an appeal to design apparently remains, even on certain versions of the many-universe hypothesis.[21] So we conclude that although the teleological argument is not conclusive, in the sense of being rationally convincing to everyone who considers it, it does have considerable force if understood as an attempt to show that the hypothesis of a designer is plausible.

But what about Hume's second set of objections? As we noted previously, Hume also objects to the argument on religious grounds.

He says that the argument does not really show that the God of theism exists. The designer of the world might in many ways fail to resemble the God of Christianity, Judaism and Islam. The designer might not be truly omnipotent in power, knowledge or goodness, but limited in various ways.[22] Indeed, says Hume, the designer might not be a single being but a committee.

Richard Swinburne has responded to these objections by claiming that the hypothesis of theism is more probable than the "finite god(s)" Hume considers, because theism is simpler.[23] The fact that the laws of nature, which bring about the order of the universe, seem universal points to one cause rather than many. Swinburne says that it is simpler to hypothesize a God with infinite power and knowledge than a god with great, though limited, powers. The hypothesis of a *limited* god would inevitably raise the question of why this being has just the amount of power and knowledge that he does—a question that would be unanswerable.

But even if Swinburne is right, Hume's objections do, nonetheless, diminish the certainty of the conclusion of an argument which was only probable in the beginning. But this simply shows that the teleological argument, like the cosmological argument, is limited in what it conveys about God. A reasonable person who accepted the argument would hardly be content with the knowledge of God thereby gained, but he would be eager to learn more about God. Natural theology, even if successful, is not supposed to give the kind of detailed knowledge of God to be gained from possible special revelations and religious experiences.

To a certain extent, however, the defects of the cosmological and teleological arguments cancel each other out. The cosmological argument concludes that a necessary being who is the cause of the universe must exist, but it does not, on its face, show that this cause must be personal. The teleological argument attempts to show that the cause of the universe must be intelligent and therefore personal, but it does not, on its face, show that this being must be a necessary being. Clearly, the two arguments complement each other and therefore could be viewed not as separate arguments but as parts of a general case for the plausibility of theism.

Someone might claim, of course, that the conclusions of the two arguments refer to two different beings and that the arguments thus cannot be used together. Here one could reply, in the spirit of Swinburne, that this seems logically possible but not plausible. It seems far-fetched to suppose that the being responsible for the very existence of the natural order would not also be ultimately responsible for its special, pervasive characteristics.

Nevertheless, if one asks whether the teleological argument is a proof of God's existence, in the sense of being rationally convincing to all, the answer must surely be negative. But perhaps that conclusion merely shows how high are the standards set by this notion of "proof"—so high, perhaps, that a proof of theism is in principle unattainable. Perhaps no significant claims in philosophy can be proven, in this sense; if this is so, the failure to prove God's existence surely is no point in favor of atheism.

Moral Arguments

The roots of the moral argument go back, philosophically, to Plato's conviction that the source of all reality and truth must be the "Form of the Good" and, religiously, to the biblical teaching that moral obligations must be understood in terms of their connection to God's requirements of us. Although not popular among philosophers, this argument probably is more convincing to "ordinary people" (nonphilosophers) than any other. The voice of conscience is still regarded by many as the voice of God.

The fact that the argument is not so popular among philosophers as it is among nonphilosophers might appear to count strongly against it, but this may not be so. Fashions come and go in philosophy, as in any other field, so the fact that an argument is not currently fashionable is not itself terribly significant. It is plausible to think, however, that *if* there is a God, and if it is important for human beings to know about him, then God would make it possible for ordinary people to know about him. That the moral argument is often convincing to unsophisticated people, while not itself impressive evidence for its truth, certainly does not count against it.

Kant developed a type of moral argument in the late-eighteenth century, but his argument was unusual in several ways.[24] Kant did not claim that the existence of morality was theoretical evidence for the truth of theism but rather that the situation of a human being who is under moral obligation as a rational, practical being makes it necessary for that person to *postulate* God's existence. The underlying insight seems to be this: it is unreasonable to try to realize moral ideals in the universe if the universe, and the laws whereby results in it are achieved, are indifferent to morality. The rational moral agent must see the universe as the arena for moral endeavor and so must believe that a moral reality lies behind the natural order. In summary, it is reasonable for one to heed reason's demand to behave morally only if we live in a moral universe, so the requirements of reason demand that we live in a moral universe, and since the idea that we live in a moral universe makes sense only if God exists, we have *rational* reasons—"rational" in that they emerge from the requirements of reason—for belief in God.

More theoretical versions of the moral argument were popular in the late-nineteenth and twentieth centuries. One of the most popular presentations of the argument is found in the apologetic work of the British professor of English C. S. Lewis, who employed the argument in his book *Mere Christianity*, as well as in other places.[25]

Like the teleological argument, the moral argument is best construed as an argument for God's existence by way of inference to the best explanation. The basic idea is that God's existence provides the most probable or plausible explanation of a certain fact: in this case, the existence of moral obligations. A simple version might go like this:

(1) (Probably) unless there is a God, there cannot be objectively binding moral obligations.

(2) There are objectively binding moral obligations.
(3) Therefore (probably) there is a God.

Many people find the argument unconvincing because they reject premise (2), claiming that there are no objectively binding moral obligations. Propositions like "A person is obligated to tell the truth even when it does not benefit him" can, of course, be interpreted in a variety of ways. One of the more popular views is that of *cultural relativism,* which interprets moral obligations in terms of social approval and disapproval. Every society approves and disapproves of particular actions, and expresses that approval and disapproval by training the young to think of those actions as "right" or "wrong." Which acts are designated right or wrong differs from culture to culture. Therefore, there are no transcendent moral obligations for God's existence (or his requirements) to explain. Morality is completely a product of human culture.

Cultural relativism faces some severe problems. First, it may be that the cultural relativist exaggerates the degree of relativism found among different cultures. There are widespread similarities in basic moral beliefs in cultures all over the world. This is particularly true if one recognizes that a great deal of what appears to be moral disagreement may actually be a disagreement about nonmoral facts. Two cultures might agree that it would be a bad thing to kill and eat the members of one's family, but one culture might believe that one risks doing so in slaughtering and eating a cow (who might be the reincarnation of a deceased loved one), while the other culture believes that there is no such possibility. Hence, one culture regards the eating of beef to be immoral, while the other does not. In this case, the disagreement is not over the moral issue of whether it is permissible to kill and eat one's loved ones, but rather the factual issue of whether reincarnation (of a certain variety) is true.

More to the point though, the existence of moral disagreements among cultures, regardless of how prevalent it is, does not entail that there is no objective moral truth. Suppose culture X says that action A is right, while culture Y says action A is wrong. Why should we conclude from this that A is neither objectively right nor objectively wrong? Would it not be more reasonable to infer that one culture is right and the other culture mistaken? Alternatively, both cultures could be mistaken, or both partially right. In any case, relativity in moral beliefs and practices does not imply that moral *truth* is relative.

The most serious problem with cultural relativism is that it makes it impossible to evaluate cultures morally. Since there is no higher moral standard than culture, one cannot criticize as immoral that which is approved in a particular culture, even if the culture approves of infanticide, racism or genocide. To see how disturbing this is, consider a culture such as Nazi Germany. Who can accept the claim that Hitler—who acted within the standards of Nazi culture—was not immoral? Cultural relativism also makes the whole idea of moral progress impossible. The idea of moral progress presupposes that it is possible for some practices to be truly better than others.

Another popular way of rejecting our second premise is to accept an even more extreme relativism: *individual relativism.* On this view, whatever the individual accepts as right is right for her. A view which is theoretically different but has the same practical result is ethical *emotivism.* The emotivist says that there are no real (that is, objectively binding) moral obligations. When a person says that an act is wrong, she is not stating a fact, but only expressing her individual emotions or attitude about the act.

It is extremely difficult in practice to hold consistently to any form of relativism or emotivism. It is easy enough to say that there are no real moral obligations, but most people cannot help believing that when they are wronged by someone else, the act really is wrong. If a person maliciously trips you and then laughs because you have cut your lip, it will seem to you that the person has wronged you and that it is an objective *fact* that he has done so. It is no good to say that the person who tripped you *thought* the act was right and therefore, for him, it *was* right. The act was wrong, and the person *should* have recognized this and regretted the act, even if he felt no such emotion. The person who did the tripping is likely to say the same thing when he is tripped.

So far, we have been examining those views that criticize the argument by rejecting premise (2): "There are objectively binding moral obligations." What about premise (1): "(Probably) unless there is a God, there cannot be objectively binding moral obligations"? Some nontheists, such as Sartre, have accepted this premise, agreeing with Ivan in *The Brothers Karamazov* that "if there is no God, then everything is permitted." Sartre agrees that there can be no objective moral obligations without God, and he therefore tries to ground morality in the personal choices of the individual, which appears to be a form of individual relativism.

Other nontheists, however, are unwilling to concede premise (1). Naturalistic humanism, for example, tries to show that moral obligations can exist even if there is no God. This can be done in two ways: (1) one can claim that the existence of moral obligations is simply an ultimate fact which needs no explanation; (2) one can try to give a naturalistic explanation for the existence of moral obligations. The latter is the more popular alternative.

It is impossible to survey briefly all the alternative ways naturalists have tried to explain morality, but these are three of the more common views: first, moral obligations are grounded in self-interest; second, moral obligations are grounded in natural instinct; and third, moral obligations can be explained as a result of evolution. We will briefly consider each of these views in turn.

The first view basically boils down to the claim that morality "pays": one should be moral *because* it is in one's own, personal best interest to be moral. (The "because" is important here: many alternative views include the claim that being moral is *in fact* in one's own best interest but deny that this is *why* one should be moral or that this is the *basis* of one's moral obligations.) On this view, one should be benevolent and honest, for example, because in the long run, if one is cruel or dishonest to others, then they will most likely return the favor. Since one does not want this to happen, one must respect what others want. This view faces two major problems. First, it seems that there are at least a few cases where doing one's moral duty might require a sacrifice, such as giving one's life, which could not possibly result in a net benefit for oneself (assuming, as the naturalist does, that there is no afterlife). So morality does not always pay, even if it usually does. Second, what follows from the "self-interest" view is not that one should always want to be moral but rather that one should always want to *appear* to be moral to one's fellows. When one is sure that one can get away with it, there is no reason not to ignore one's moral obligations. Some say that morality is grounded not in what pays off for oneself but in what is best for all. But that is *part* of morality; to say morality is grounded in what is good for all is not an explanation of morality but a statement of what it is about morality that is puzzling and needs explanation. *Why* am I as an individual obligated to do what is best for all instead of what is best for just myself?

The second naturalistic position attempts to view moral obligations to help other people as based on natural instincts, such as the impulse to feel sympathy for others. Doubtless, there are such instincts, but it is hard to see how their existence could be an adequate explanation of morality. There are instincts that—regardless of how common or "natural" they may be—it seems clearly immoral for one to act upon (the instinct toward racial discrimination, for example). In fact, most people seem to experience moral obligations as requiring them frequently to override their strongest instincts. Likewise, other instincts (such as the instinct toward protecting one's child from all immediate pain and discomfort) are such that they seem to be neither wholly good nor wholly bad, and consequently, critical reflection is required to determine whether they should be followed in a particular case. But there seems to be no basis for classifying some instincts as moral and others as immoral, or some as appropriate to act upon in a given situation and others not, unless there is some higher standard for evaluating instincts. To allow for such a standard, however, is to admit that natural instincts are not the ultimate basis of morality, which amounts to abandoning the theory in question.

The third way naturalists try to explain morality is by appeal to evolutionary theory. In a nutshell, the idea is that in the course of our evolutionary development, those human beings who had the peculiar notions that they were "obligated" to be kind, helpful and so on were more likely to survive than their rivals in the process of natural selection. In this way evolution is thought to explain the ubiquity of moral *beliefs:* people who had such beliefs were more likely to survive. But it is hard to see how evolution could account for anyone's being *actually obligated.* In fact, someone who accepted this evolutionary theory could quite consistently reject the existence of actual moral obligations. (Those who do so reject the second premise of the moral argument and thus need not reject the first premise to avoid the argument's conclusion. In this case, however, they will face many of the same problems as the relativist.)

The heart of the moral argument, then, is the intuition that there would be something very odd about the existence of moral obligations in a naturalistic universe. How, in a world which is ultimately the product of time, chance and material particles, did there come to be such things as moral obligations? Perhaps the strongest response of the naturalist is simply to insist that moral obligations are another brute fact. But this would certainly seem to be an odd kind of brute fact in a *naturalistic* universe. In the judgment of many theists, the existence of moral truths is something that needs to be *explained*, and no naturalistic account is able to do so adequately.

But in what way, exactly, is it thought that God's existence explains the existence of moral obligations? How does it remove or lessen this oddity? Here, theists have given a variety of answers. One of the most prominent answers, especially among Protestant Christians, is that moral obligations are grounded in divine commands, such that, without God to issue commands, there would be no moral obligations. *Divine command theories* can be developed in two general ways. The more ambitious way seeks to ground the existence of both moral goodness and moral obligation in divine commands. This view is open to several serious—and interrelated—objections. First, it appears to render God's commands arbitrary: God cannot command us to do what is right either because it *is* right or because it *is* good, since both qualities are determined by God's act of commanding. The view thus implies that God has no more reason to command loving one's neighbor than hating or murdering one's neighbor; either would be equally good and right, were God to command it. Thus, God lacks moral reasons for commanding one thing rather than another; his commands are arbitrary. This, in turn, further implies that God could make absolutely any action—say, torturing and murdering babies for fun—morally obligatory, just by commanding it. Finally, the view also trivializes divine goodness: it appears that God would qualify as perfectly good no matter what he had chosen to do or command.

A more defensible version of divine command theory, then, must be less ambitious in what it seeks to explain. Many contemporary divine command theorists hold that God's commanding an action does not make the action good—the action has this property independent of divine commands—but it makes it morally *obligatory* for humans. God recognizes what is good and commands us to do it; his commanding us to do it creates an obligation for us to do what is antecedently good.[26] This version of divine command theory thus needs to be supplemented by some independent theory of goodness in order for one to have a complete theory of value.[27]

Other theists reject divine command theory as an explanation of morality, although they would agree that God commands us to do what is right. They argue, instead, that morality must somehow be rooted in the nature of things. According to theistic *human nature theories*, in order to understand our obligations, we must understand the human telos, which, in theistic terms, is the divinely intended purpose for which we were created. Human beings have intrinsic worth in virtue of the way we have been created by God (e.g., in virtue of being created in God's image). Consequently, there are specific ways that human beings should—and should not—be treated. Our moral obligations to other people are defined by what promotes and allows us to achieve, individually and collectively, human flourishing. God has created us with moral faculties such that, simply by reflecting carefully on human nature, we are able to discern God's intentions for how we are to treat other people. In principle then our moral obligations could be "read off" from a complete and accurate description of human nature. However, in light of the fact that many people's rational faculties are rather limited—not to mention the fact that human moral faculties in general are partially corrupted by sin—God has revealed many of these obligations to us in the form of commands. But divine commands on this view simply reveal to us what we are antecedently obligated to do, rather than bringing into existence moral obligations.

Each view has its advantages. For example, a divine command theory has the advantage of being able to account for individual obligations—obligations binding on some particular person or group but not on others—because it allows that God can bring new obligations into existence simply by issuing commands, and God can restrict the scope of certain commands, if he so chooses. It seems doubtful that a human nature theory can accommodate such obligations. But human nature theories may have an advantage in being able to account for moral obligations that are binding on us prior to and independently of God's issuing any commands. This might be useful—for example, in a discussion of a contemporary ethical issue like cloning—because it affords one the resources to argue for the existence of obligations that one is unable to trace back to any specific command that God has given us.

Many other ways of grounding morality in God are possible. All would agree that the existence of moral obligations makes more sense in a universe in which the ultimate reality is a moral person than it does in a universe where persons are a late and insignificant byproduct of impersonal forces. Much of morality is simply a matter of respecting the worth and value of persons, and that seems more reasonable in a universe which is ultimately "personal."

Like the other arguments we have discussed, the moral argument is certainly not rationally convincing to everyone who considers it. Obviously, we have not shown conclusively that relativism is false or that it is impossible for the naturalist to give an explanation of moral obligations. But, once more, it seems that the moral argument does have force, at least for those who hold certain views in ethics.

It is also worthy of note that the conclusion of the argument once more complements the conclusion of the cosmological and teleological arguments. A God who provides the basis for moral obligations must be understood as a moral being, a being who cares deeply about the realization of moral values. This is something that could hardly be inferred from the other two arguments.

Conclusions: The Value of Theistic Argument

In looking at these arguments we have concluded that none of them can be judged to be a successful proof of God's existence in the sense of being rationally convincing to everyone. Whether the arguments are rationally convincing to a particular person depends in each case on whether that person is willing to accept some key premise or premises which are neither self-evident nor absolutely certain. On the other hand, we have found that there is much to be said for some of these debatable premises and that many people claim to know them to be true or at least see them as more reasonable than the alternatives. It would seem then that such arguments, individually and especially collectively, could form a case for the reasonableness of theism, at least relative to its rivals.

If these conclusions are correct, they are also significant. However, their importance should not be exaggerated. For one, there is a prominent counterview, called *Reformed epistemology,* which contends that the arguments of natural theology are unnecessary to justify religious belief. We will save discussion of Reformed epistemology for chapter eight. Even if it turns out that natural theology plays an essential role in justifying religious belief, however, it still faces a huge limitation in that, by itself, it would leave us a great deal to learn about God's nature and doings. A person content with the meager knowledge of God gained by these arguments would be too easily satisfied. Another limitation is that natural theology is highly theoretical. It seems to lead only to beliefs *about* God—that is, to propositional beliefs. On the basis of such arguments one comes only to believe that a God exists, but one does not thereby automatically acquire the kind of personal faith most religions value in speaking of faith in God (more about this in chapter eight).

By itself, then, natural theology appears somewhat deficient as a means of discovering God's reality, operating as it does on the level of theoretical inference and hypothesis, despite its usefulness in demonstrating the rational defensibility of theism. Perhaps one would be more likely to gain a living faith in God, as well as a more detailed knowledge of God, if one had some direct experience of God or if God were to reveal himself to humans in some special way. Aquinas, one of the greatest philosophical champions of natural theology, shares this estimation of the value of natural theology:

> If the only way open to us for the knowledge of God were solely that of the reason, the human race would remain in the blackest shadows of ignorance. For then the knowledge of God, which especially renders men perfect and good, would come to be possessed only by a few, and these few would require a great deal of time in order to reach it.[28]

Thus the limitations of natural theology prompt us to a consideration of religious experience and special revelation—matters to which we will now turn our attention.

4

Religious Experience

There are lots of ways to approach the reasonableness of theistic belief. One might try to isolate a set of beliefs about God from the more detailed beliefs of the world's religions and consider the merits of these core beliefs independently of the truth of any particular religion. This basically is the project of natural theology. However, it also seems possible for a person to come to believe in God as a result of coming to believe in the truth of Christianity or some other particular religion.

How might this occur? Christianity, Judaism and Islam are all religions which emphasize that human beings—at least some of them—have had experiences of God or special experiences which teach them about God. Prophets and other holy men and women have had encounters with the divine—visions, voices and inspired utterances. To consider this second route to knowing about God, it is therefore necessary to examine the related topics of religious experience and special revelation. We shall do this here and in chapter five.

Types of Religious Experience

It is important to recognize that the topic of religious experience is not limited to consideration of exceptional or mystical experiences. Genuine believers in God often feel that they "have dealings with

God" continually in their day-to-day lives. Some people seem to experience almost everything "spiritually." Daily bread may be received with gratitude, as a gift; illness may be perceived as a form of testing or even punishment.

To highlight the way religious conviction can inform the whole of experience, it is helpful to speak of the religious dimension of experience and not only of religious experiences. For some people the religious dimension of experience looms large. Perhaps there is a minor religious dimension to almost everyone's experience. We have suggested that this religious dimension of experience figures heavily in the classical theistic arguments for God's existence. The person who finds the cosmological argument convincing experiences the finite objects in the world (and herself) as radically contingent, proclaiming their dependence on a higher power. The person who finds the teleological argument convincing experiences nature as an orderly, purposeful reality where the good and beauty which are realized are no accident. The person who finds the moral argument convincing perceives certain situations as placing him under objective obligation and interprets "being morally obligated" as involving a relation between finite persons and a supreme person.

But in addition to what we have called the religious dimension of experience, there are also special experiences that are properly termed "religious." Actually, a tremendous variety of diverse experiences are designated as "religious." Before any useful analysis of such experiences can be given, some of the different types must be sorted out so that it is reasonably clear what kind of experience one is talking about.

One important distinction is that between the kind of religious experience in which the individual experiences union with the divine and that in which the individual experiences a separation between himself and God. Many people, spontaneously or as a result of long training and discipline, seem to have experiences in which they become aware of a profound unity underlying all things. Sometimes this unity or oneness is seen as total and absolute; the distinctions and differences which are part of ordinary experience drop out or are perceived as less than fully real—or even as wholly illusory. This unity is thus regarded as the ultimate reality, what is truly divine. The proponent of ***absolute monism*** claims that everything, at bottom, is part of this one reality, particularly one's own soul or consciousness: in the words of the Hindu *Upanishads*, "That thou art." This experience of union with the divine is seen as revelatory and liberating.

One would expect such experiences to figure prominently in pantheistic or panentheistic religions, and this is correct. Such experiences are not always interpreted monistically or pantheistically, however. The theist also believes that God is a unitary reality that underlies everything that exists, including the human self. Orthodox theists tend to interpret such experiences as experiences of God, with the proviso that the union between God and other things is never total or absolute. Even within Hinduism there are prominent thinkers who understand God or Brahman as ultimately a personal reality who therefore cannot be absolutely identified with his creatures, even though he is one with them in a real sense.[1] Other theists interpret the absolute monistic type of experience not as an experience of God but as an awareness of the soul as pure selfhood or consciousness, stripped of all particular qualities.

The experience of union with the divine is sometimes designated as "mystical experience" and contrasted with an experience in which God's separateness or otherness is powerfully brought to the fore. The latter kind of experience is then described as "numinous," to use the term of Rudolf Otto, who gave a classical description of such experiences in his book *The Idea of the Holy*. Others use the term "mysticism" in a broader sense, describing the two types of experiences as monistic mysticism and theistic mysticism.

We should stress that the experience of the numinous does not necessarily exclude any sense of oneness. Although the dominant element in the numinous type of experience is an awareness of God's greatness and one's own insignificance or impurity in relation to

God, the numinous experience may also include a sense of one's connectedness with God. Otto himself stresses the ambivalent nature of the experience. God is seen as a reality that is both terrifying and fascinating, the object of desire and of a kind of fear or dread. A classical example is Isaiah's vision of the Lord lifted up, high and mighty—a vision that inspired Isaiah to cry out, "Woe is me! I am lost, for I am a man of unclean lips" (Is 6:5 NRSV).

Perhaps we could characterize religious experience in general terms simply as purported awareness of the divine. The typical elements in religious experience are three: a sense of *union* with the divine, a sense of *dependence* on the divine and a sense of *separateness* from the divine. Pantheistic and monistic mystical experiences emphasize the first of these elements. Theistic experience usually includes all three elements, though one element may be dominant. Thus, theists have mystical experiences in which the dominant theme is a sense of oneness with the divine. Theists also have numinous experiences in which the dominant theme is a sense of radical separation from God, who is perceived as a fearsome yet attractive reality.

This distinction is by no means hard and fast. In fact, most "ordinary" theistic religious experiences probably include both mystical and numinous elements, though the "unity" side of the experience is not typically interpreted monistically as an *absolute* unity. Rather, the theist claims to enjoy an experienced union with God of the sort that is possible between two persons who are united in love and devotion. But this unity is qualified by an awareness of the great gulf between humans and God, creatures and Creator, as well as the great gulf between sinful creatures and an absolutely *holy* being.

Since our main focus in this book is on the reasonableness of theistic-type religions, we shall concentrate in what follows on theistic-type experiences. The experience of the absolute monist is an interesting field of study, but also an exceptionally difficult one, especially because the monist so often insists that his experience defies description and analysis. The experience of "oneness" that is so characteristic of mysticism, in any case, seems to be capable of various interpretations, some of which are compatible with theism. It seems unlikely, then, that the mystical type of experience could be used to justify theism over against its rivals, but it is also unlikely that such experiences could undermine the reasonableness of theistic belief.

In discussing theistic experience it is helpful to distinguish experiences that, on their face, are supernatural and miraculous from those that are more ordinary. Many people claim to have seen visions or heard voices which they took to be of God. Others claim to have heard or seen angels, the Virgin Mary or some notable saint. Experiences such as these raise special problems; for now, our attention will be on what may be termed "ordinary theistic experience."

Two Models for Understanding Experience

Before analyzing theistic experience, we need first to get clearer about what it means, in general, to experience something. The term "experience" is not very precise or clear in ordinary usage. It is sometimes used to designate an episode in which a person is aware of some reality existing independently of herself. "Susan heard the office manager speak" and "Jim saw the foreman walk out the door" are typical examples of experiences in this sense. However, the term "experience" is also used sometimes to designate a psychological process or subjective mental state of a person, which may or may not be caused by anything existing independently of the person. On this usage Jim's experience of seeing the foreman walk out the door consists of a set of visual and auditory events occurring as part of Jim's mental history.

It is crucial to note that, on the second usage of the term, to say that a person has an experience does not imply that what he experiences has any independent reality. Thus, in the case of Jim's "seeing" the foreman, if Jim is having a hallucination, then his experience could be subjectively the same as in a case of normal perception. "Experience" here refers to the subjective images and sensations, which may occur without their objective counterparts.

Some experiences clearly seem to be subjective in this way. Dreams are paradigmatic examples of such subjective experiences. The experiences, in this case, clearly are mental episodes which do not represent any mind-independent reality. These cases are fairly uncontroversial. The interesting cases are the ones where the person seems to be aware of something existing objectively or independently. Her subjective episodes purport to represent some objective reality.

Some philosophers, drawing on the second usage of the term "experience," have insisted that a person never has a direct encounter or awareness of the external world. Rather, our experience is limited to our own private sensations and images. When a person sees a tree, what he really sees is not the actual tree but a set of images or sensations produced by his brain as a result of the appropriate sensory input. The subjective image then serves as a representation of the actual tree in the physical world. This way of looking at experience we shall term *the representational model.* The alternative view, which draws on the other sense of "experience," is the model of *direct realism.* This view claims that in cases of genuine perceptual experience, a person is directly aware of what she sees or hears. Thus, if the foreman was not present when Jim claimed to see him, then Jim did not really see him at all. Jim thought he was seeing the foreman, but he was mistaken. The direct realist model thus takes it to be the case that if Jim experiences X, then X must exist.

The direct realist claims that an experience of an object provides evidence of an impressive sort for the object's reality. On the representational model, however, the move from having an experience of an object to belief in the reality of the object is a little more indirect. Since we do not experience the object directly, it is often claimed that a kind of inference is required. The representationalist may reason as follows: I am having the experience (subjective sensations) I call "seeing a tree." Normally, these sensations are caused by there being a tree present to me. Therefore, probably there is a tree present to me.

Many analyses of religious experience follow this representational model. Thus, religious experiences are viewed as subjective sensations that occur in the believer. As such, the existence of religious experiences is undeniable. The difficult question, however, is to decide what, if anything, can be inferred from the occurrence of such sensations. Often, the argument proceeds in terms of a debate about the causes of such experiences. Take, for example, a conversion experience in which a person feels an intense sense of forgiveness, acceptance and wholeness. That these sensations are really present in the believer no one will deny, but the believer will say that the cause of the feelings is God's activity, while the skeptic will claim that these psychological changes can be explained naturalistically.

It is difficult to see how one could resolve such disputes. The matter is made more complicated in that it is not clear that natural psychological processes always (or ever) invalidate theistic explanations, since God as the Creator is responsible for natural processes and can accomplish his ends through them. Hence it is not clear that the naturalistic causes invoked by the skeptic invalidate a religious explanation. (More on this in chapter six.) However, it still may be hard for the believer to convince the skeptic, who sees no explanatory need for anything beyond the natural world, that it is necessary to posit God as the cause of the psychological states in question.

The difficulty in using religious experience to justify religious beliefs on this representational model may, however, be due more to the model and the way it is being employed than to any special problems with religious experience. It is instructive here to look at the results of applying the representational model of experience to other areas. If one consistently holds to a representational view of experience and claims that the knowledge of the external world *always* depends on an inference of some kind, then grave problems appear. For if we are limited to experience of subjective sensations and *never* have any direct awareness of the objective reality that presumably causes those sensations, then how can we infer anything about that reality from the occurrence of the sensations? We would in that case have no way of testing rival hypotheses about the causes of sensations. The only way to avoid skepticism would seem to be to assume that the real world usually is as it appears to be; the causes of our perceptions of objects such as trees and stones are trees and stones. It is hard to see why religious believers attracted to a representational model of experience should not make a similar assumption. What appears to be the activity of God is, normally at least, the activity of God.

To avoid such problems with respect to ordinary perceptual experience, many philosophers are attracted to the model of direct realism. The direct-realist model appears to be a promising one for analyzing theistic experiences, as well. Theists often claim to be aware of God's presence, of his love and forgiveness. They may claim to have an awareness of God's providential guidance or of God's holiness or majesty. We shall try now to examine such theistic experiences on a direct-realist model.

Experience of God as Direct and Mediated

The claim that people may have direct experiences of God has often been rejected as impossible, but the reasons commonly advanced for this rejection are not very good ones. Some claim that it is impossible for a finite being to experience an infinite being.[2] Why? Perhaps it is reasonable to claim that a finite being's experience of an infinite being could never be exhaustive or complete, but is evidently compatible with some kind of genuine awareness. One's own experience need not *be* infinite in order to experience an infinitely powerful being, just as a person can observe a sad person without being sad herself.

Other people claim that the only proper objects of experience are sensory qualities. By "sensory qualities," they mean, in this context, qualities like being red, yellow or blue, hard or soft, warm or cold—qualities clearly associated with a specific sensory organ. If the proper objects of experience are such sensory qualities, then one might argue that one cannot directly experience God, since it is implausible to regard God as a sensory quality or collection of such qualities.

The doctrine that we can only experience these kinds of sensory qualities is a dubious one. In ordinary speech, people commonly talk about experiencing many things—such as heroic deeds, loving gestures, historically significant artifacts—which are not simply collections of sensory qualities. The proponent of the doctrine that we only experience sensory qualities must claim that we do not directly experience such things; we experience other things—colors, noises and so on—which are *interpreted* as the objects we take them to be. But to this the response can be made that often there seems to be no interpretation going on at all. In fact, it often seems to be the case that one can recognize an object as an object of a particular kind without being able to say what sensory qualities make possible the identification. One may see a woman whom one recognizes as one's sister without being able to describe precisely or even vaguely the sensory qualities that enable one to distinguish her from a woman with a similar physical appearance. Distinguishing between what is "really experienced" and the interpretation of experience is none too easy.

Even if one manages to draw a clear line between "raw experience" and "interpretation," which seems unlikely, it is not evident that this will be prejudicial to the case for religious experience. Most important experiences which we take as evidence of what the world is like will, on this view, probably contain an element of interpretation. If this is so, then the fact that religious experiences also contain an interpretive element will not necessarily make them less reliable than other significant kinds of experience. Most experience is experiencing something *as* something. Recognition involves the perception of a thing under some category or concept, a skill which must be learned and, in some cases, even requires special training. (Consider the training required by a microbiologist to recognize the pattern of shapes and colors viewed through a microscope *as* a particular strain of E. coli bacteria, for example.) It should not be thought surprising or damaging, then, that much religious experience is like this as well.

There is a third objection to the thesis that people might directly experience God, and perhaps it is present as the concealed ground of the first two objections we have considered. It is difficult for some people to understand how an immaterial being like God can be *directly* perceived. They might admit that one could experience something that is an effect of God's activity, but not God himself. Suppose, for example, that one heard a voice from the sky saying, "This is the Lord speaking." Surely it is most reasonable to think that what is directly heard in this case are sound waves that God has caused to occur, not God himself.

The first thing to say about this objection is that it proves too much. It would follow that in an ordinary conversation with another person what one hears is not the other person talking but rather only the sound waves that the person causes with his voice. This helps to highlight what is wrong with the objection. When we speak of direct experience of something, we do not mean that the experience is completely unmediated. The directness is a psychological feature of the experience, and it is compatible with there being a complicated and indirect process which is, in some sense, responsible for the experience.[3] Much confusion here results from conflating the description of an experience as it is experienced with the causal explanation of what makes the experience possible. When a person gazes out a window and sees a lovely elm tree, the experience may be perfectly direct. No inference or interpretation need be present to consciousness at all. The person just sees the tree and therefore has good reason to believe a tree is there. All this is compatible with a complicated story of how the experience takes place, a story involving the reflection of light rays and the operations of the eye and the brain. The person sees the tree through the operation of a complex causal chain which constitutes a medium, but he is not necessarily experiencing that medium. He may know nothing about light rays or how the retina and optic nerves function.

In general, then, it is possible to have an experience of something which is psychologically direct but still involves a complex causal process. If one tries to rule out as not being direct any experience involving mediating processes, it seems likely that, in the end, no experience at all will qualify as direct. It is also noteworthy that human beings are not limited to their own sensory organs as media for perceiving objects. People often perceive things through rather extended media, such as reflecting telescopes and telephones. A person who hears a friend talk over the phone really can hear the friend, even though the medium in this case involves electronic signals transmitted over wires.

Though we would not wish to rule out dogmatically the possibility of an unmediated experience of God—this may be what mystical experience is all about—it seems to us that most experiences that purport to be experiences of God fall into this category of direct, though mediated, experience. Since God, if he exists, is the ultimate cause of the existence of everything in the natural world, it does not seem impossible to experience God through some other object. Nor does the complexity of the causal process thereby imply that the experience cannot be psychologically direct.

Believers in God, in any case, do commonly describe God's speaking to them *through* the voice of a preacher or *through* the words of a hymn. They may speak of experiencing God's presence *in* the closeness of a friend's embrace or *in* the beauty of a majestic sunset. God may speak through the words of a sacred book or poem. Such experiences can be psychologically direct; the experiencer may have no awareness at all of making any inference or interpretation. Such cases are plausibly analyzed as cases of direct, though mediated, experiences of God. The individual takes herself to experience God in and through something else that is experienced.

In his book *Belief in God*, George Mavrodes points out an interesting feature of mediated experiences that seems applicable to religious experience. In cases where extended media are involved, such as in the example of a telephone or reflecting telescope, it is possible for two people to have the same sensory input, and yet have two different experiences. A technician who is examining a telescope mirror for flaws may gaze into a telescope and see only a mirror with various reflections. An astronomer may gaze under the same conditions and see an interesting galaxy. The one individual sees the medium; the other sees something else through the medium. What is seen depends in part on the skills and interests of the person looking.

If religious experiences occur that involve a true awareness of God, this phenomenon may partly explain why such experiences are not universally shared. Two people may hear the same sermon, but one hears only the sermon, while the other hears God speaking through the sermon. We will discuss next other possible reasons why religious experiences are not universally shared.

Are Religious Experiences Veridical?

Does anyone truly have such direct, mediated experiences of God? Philosophers call an experience in which the object of experience is being truly perceived a *veridical experience.* Are any religious experiences of the type we have been discussing veridical? The question is perfectly legitimate, because it is evident that not all experiences are veridical. Mistakes, illusions and even hallucinations do occur.

Many philosophers are skeptical of the claims of believers to have such direct experiences of God. There are many reasons for such skepticism. One, undoubtedly, is a conviction on the part of some that God does not exist. Obviously, if God does not exist, veridical experience of him is impossible. But it is hardly fair to dismiss possible evidence for God's existence on such grounds unless one really knows God does not exist. Such an objection to religious experience will only be reasonable if the objector has a strong reason to believe that God does not exist, a reason strong enough to override the evidence that religious experience itself might provide. In later chapters we will look at some arguments that have been put forward as proofs that God does not exist.

A more reasonable basis for doubt lies in the alleged failure of religious experiences to be intersubjectively verifiable. Normally, we distinguish between veridical and nonveridical experiences by comparing the experiences of various people. If someone claims to see a gremlin in her office, but none of her colleagues can perceive it, the discrepancy is evidence that she is hallucinating, seeing things which don't exist. Public checking procedures can determine whether an experience is veridical. If one is in doubt as to whether there really is a gremlin in one's office, one can try to take a picture of the creature, or one can ask others whether they see anything and, if so, what they see.

Critics claim that religious experiences lack this feature of being publicly checkable or intersubjectively verifiable. When Jack hears the voice of God in the words of the preacher, Mary hears only a boring sermon. When one soldier feels God's presence as he huddles in the foxhole, the soldier next to him feels only the cold night air. The failure of others to have the experiences and the lack of standard checking procedures are thought to undermine the credibility of the experiential claims.

The critic is quite correct here to insist on the importance of intersubjective checks on experiential claims. Some religious believers have denied the need for such checks, claiming that their experiences are in some way infallible or incorrigible. But it is difficult to see how any experience could acquire such a status and even more difficult to see how this claim could be argued or defended. If one insists too strongly on the infallibility of one's experience, one runs the danger of emptying the experience of objective status. Normally, the only experiential claims that come close to being infallible are claims about one's own, present, subjective mental states. If someone claims that the room is cold, he may be overruled by a thermometer; if he claims, sincerely, that it *feels* cold to him, his claim seems impossible to refute. But the believer wants religious experience to be more than mere subjective feelings.

One might begin to respond to the critic here by noting that, although checking procedures are important, it is reasonable to demand that they be used only in cases where there is some prima facie reason to doubt the experience. It would be unreasonable to demand that *every* experience be intersubjectively verified before being accepted, for the process of checking an experience (taking a picture, asking someone else what she saw) itself involves experiences whose reliability must be, at least provisionally, taken for granted.

Because it only makes sense to check experiences in particular cases, some philosophers accept what has been termed the *principle of credulity:* roughly, the claim that if one has an experience in which it seems that X is present and has certain features, then it is reasonable to believe that X is really present and that X has those features, unless one has some overriding reason to think that, on this occasion, one's senses may be unreliable.[4] The principle of credulity is motivated by the assumption that experience is usually or normally veridical. Things usually are as they appear to be, or, at the very least, the fact that someone experiences X provides some evidence that X is real and present. This is far from the claim that experience is infallible; it is, rather, a claim that experience provides prima facie evidence that should normally be accepted, unless one has stronger evidence that leads one to doubt or discount the experience. It is for those cases in which one has reason to doubt one's experience that checking procedures are important.

What kinds of evidence can lead us to override or question claims based on experience? Two kinds of challenges are possible. First, one might have good reason for believing that the object claimed to be experienced could not have been experienced. For example, if one knew that a unicorn did not exist, that fact would undermine any claim to see a unicorn. Alternatively, one might know that the object was not present to the person or that the person was not in the appropriate position to have had the experience claimed. For example, one would discount the testimony of a person who claimed to see an accident but was known to be in another city at the time of the accident.

The second type of challenge is an inductive argument which points out that an experience occurred in a certain situation that, in the past, has frequently produced delusory or mistaken experiential claims. One might argue, for example, that visions experienced under the influence of drugs known to cause hallucinations are not to be trusted.

It is hard to see how a successful challenge of either sort can be made against ordinary theistic experience. Since God is omnipresent, it is hard to see how one could know that a person was not in a position to experience God. Challenges of the second sort are frequently made against mystical experiences, which are alleged to be the product of unusual physical states, such as fasting. It is hard to see how the critic could know that such states are exceptionally likely to produce illusory experiences; but in any case, such objections cannot be made against ordinary theistic experiences, which often are not associated with any unusual psychological or physiological states.

It seems reasonable, therefore, to take the experiences of theists as prima facie evidence that God is indeed real, following the principle of credulity. However, even if it is difficult for a skeptic to challenge this conclusion, this does not relieve all doubts concerning the validity of such experiences. The theist's case may even appear to be too easy. The failure of the experiences to be universally shared still makes one suspicious. Regardless of the principle of credulity, many people doubt whether anyone experiences God. This is especially true of people who lack such experiences themselves, but it is sometimes also true of believers. The question then arises as to how or whether claims to experience God can be checked. Closer consideration of this question may relieve some of the suspicion about religious experiences and establish such experiences as having even more evidential value.

Checking Experiential Claims

The whole business of checking experiential claims is not so easy and straightforward as it might appear to be if we limited our attention to such easy-to-observe objects as trees or books. Even with such simple examples as these, it is obvious that certain conditions have to be fulfilled if someone is to check our experience by duplicating it.

Suppose someone observed a book in his office. For some reason, let us suppose, he questions whether the experience is veridical. The failure of someone else, who lives several hundred miles away, to see the book obviously does not pose a threat to the veridicality of his experience. To see the book in the office, a person normally must be in that office. Just as obviously, the book must be there; if one of his colleagues has borrowed it, then a failure to observe it later will not properly count against his original experience. Also, any person who hopes to duplicate his experience must have relatively normal eyesight, the light must be tolerably good and so forth. The person must also be able to recognize a book, which plausibly means that the person must have some understanding of the concept of a book.

To summarize, even in simple cases there are both objective and subjective conditions that must be satisfied for a successful observation to be carried out. Subjectively, the observer must be a qualified observer; she must have the abilities and interests that are necessary. Objectively, the object perceived and the conditions under which it is perceived must also be right. In the case of objects like bacteria seen through a microscope or wild animals observed by a trained zoologist, these conditions may be very complicated. It may, in fact, be impossible to specify them precisely and completely. Obviously, in such a situation, the failure of someone to reduplicate an experience does not necessarily mean that the original experience was illusory.

The situation with respect to experiencing God seems similarly complicated. The failure of some people to have religious experiences may cast *some* doubt on the reliability of the experiences. But this fact would only be a *decisive* problem if it were likely that the objective and subjective conditions for successful perception had been met.

What are these conditions for religious experiences? It is difficult to say, precisely. Whether a person is a qualified observer, in this case, may turn on many factors. First, the individual may have to be attentive; he may have to be looking for God. Since we are considering mediated experiences, it is well to recall that in such cases two people with different interests can receive the same sensory input, one perceiving something through the medium and the other seeing only the medium. Second, certain kinds of recognition skills may be necessary; the person may need to be taught how to recognize God's activity. Third, religious people commonly claim that the quality of one's life or character affects one's ability to see God. Honesty, sincerity and a love for goodness and holiness are often claimed to be important factors.

The importance of these subjective factors is at least part of what is meant by those religions, notably Christianity, which emphasize the necessity of faith to know God truly. Most Christians believe that God wants human beings to freely choose to serve and obey him out of love, not out of fear of his power or a desire for selfish rewards. If God's reality were too obvious, it would be difficult for even selfish men and women to avoid obeying his laws, for it would be the height of foolishness to knowingly challenge an omnipotent, omniscient being. It makes sense, therefore, that God would make his presence known to people in such a way that those who do not wish to serve and obey him could remain ignorant of his reality. Given the complexity and deviousness of the human psyche, it is difficult to say who is a true seeker after God, and therefore difficult to say who is a qualified observer.

It is, if anything, even more difficult to say when the objective conditions for experiencing God have been satisfied. The difficulty is that God is not a passive object to be observed. He is like Aslan in C. S. Lewis's Narnia books; Aslan is "not a tame lion." Things like trees and books just sit there, waiting to be seen. People and animals have some initiative. If they do not want to be seen, they can hide and make things difficult for a would-be observer. God, however, being omnipotent and perfectly free, has the greatest possible degree of initiative. It seems impossible that anyone should experience God unless God wills it to occur. And it seems difficult or impossible for us to say when God will do this.

The fact that God must in some sense take the initiative if true awareness of him is to occur is doubtless what leads religious people to talk of the knowledge of God as coming through revelation. If the previous remarks are correct, then any veridical experience of God is a revelation, a self-revealing act on God's part.

The skeptic may here retort that God would presumably want everyone to know about himself and should therefore be expected to reveal himself to all. The believer's response to this is that God has revealed himself to all; a general revelation of God is available in nature and in conscience. But God, being a particular person and not "being-itself," can also reveal himself selectively and specially. He calls Abraham to a foreign country; he speaks to Moses in the burning bush. God's actions here are mysterious to us, and it would be folly to attempt to specify the conditions under which God will act to reveal himself. On the whole, then, the failure of some people to reduplicate the experiences of religious believers does not count very much against the veridicality of such experiences, because it is not possible to specify the conditions under which a successful observation could be predicted with any degree of certainty.

In this discussion we have been assuming that it is not possible for others to verify experiences of God. But this may be an unwarranted assumption. In reality, religious believers typically do assume that it is possible for others to reduplicate their experiences. Often they go to great lengths to invite others to share their experiences. They attempt to get other people to assume the proper attitude; they show them "where to look" and teach them to recognize God when he is present. And often they seem to be successful in this: there is a good deal of agreement among religious people about what God is like and under what circumstances he can be discovered.

Indeed, the existence of the community of religious believers who claim to have experience of God may even provide evidence of God's reality for those who personally do not have such experiences. A good deal of what humans know is not gained through firsthand experience but through the testimony of others. Why should this not be the case for religious knowledge as well?

5

Special Acts of God: Revelation and Miracles

Since whether a person experiences God will depend partly on whether God wills that to happen, every genuine experience of God is a revelation, a self-revealing act on the part of God. Theologians have traditionally claimed that God has revealed himself in two ways: generally, through his creation, but also in particular ways, to particular people, at particular points in time. The former is *general revelation* (or *natural revelation*) and is the area of concern of natural theology. The latter is referred to as *special revelation* because here God acts "specially"—that is, not merely as he always does. Judaism, Christianity and Islam have always claimed that the teachings of certain prophets or holy people constituted special revelation. When put into written form and invested with special authority, such teachings then become the basis for what is termed *revealed theology.*

Special Acts

The idea that God reveals himself in such particular ways, while implicit in the account of religious experience given in the last chapter, is by no means uncontroversial. It clearly presupposes a highly personal God, a God capable of authorizing certain people to be prophets or of selecting a certain nation to be a chosen people. For Christians, God's special activity culminates in his actually becoming a particular person in history.

People who find the conception of God as personal too limiting will have difficulty accepting such claims. Although God is not merely "one more being," on the traditional view, he is clearly a particular being who has distinctive characteristics and performs particular actions. He does not merely hold the world in existence and maintain the laws of nature. To use a commercial metaphor, God's actions are performed not merely at the wholesale level but the retail as well.

The subject of special revelation is essentially an extension of the topic of religious experience. The major difference between this chapter and the last is that, in this chapter we will be considering the possibility that some of God's revealing acts could have a particular authority for the believer, and we will give extended consideration to the difficulties involved in believing that God performs "special actions"—as well as to the difficulties involved in recognizing such actions. This is essentially the problem of whether it is reasonable to believe in miracles and, if so, what miracles it is reasonable to accept.

The topics of special revelation and miracles are connected in a variety of ways. First, on many accounts, special revelations of God *are* a type of miracle. It is typical of a believer to claim that the words of the prophets or of holy books were the result of divine inspiration. Such revelations are not seen as events that can be given a completely naturalistic explanation. So if miracles are impossible, special revelation in at least one sense will also be impossible.

Second, miracles usually are a type of special revelation, or at least they can function as such. We will consider various definitions of "miracle" later, but, on some definitions, miracles are seen as acts of God that are of evidently divine origin, acts in which God reveals himself in a unique manner.

Third, the writings which are claimed to be special revelations by Judaism, Christianity and Islam contain accounts of many purported miracles. Unless it is reasonable to believe in miracles, it will not be reasonable to think that these revelations are completely trustworthy. It will be necessary to "demythologize" them.

Fourth, since few people have personal experience of miracles, the evidential relation may also go the other way. The evidence for miracles may consist chiefly in the testimony for them that is contained in special revelation. The reasonableness of belief in specific miracles may then depend on the reasonableness of regarding a certain revelation as having special authority.

We shall begin by considering various views of revelation, some of which attempt to interpret revelation such that its miraculous character is eliminated or made unnecessary. After criticism of some of these rival views, we shall return to a more traditional view and then further explore the general problem of miracles.

Theories of Revelation

Within the Christian tradition three major views of revelation have emerged. These views have counterparts in other religions as well. Hence, although the following focuses on the problems of revelation as they have been faced by Christians, the discussion has relevance to followers of other religions as well, since these other believers face analogous problems. Such a brief account as will be given here will require overgeneralization and simplification. Each of the three views is capable of more varied and subtle development than this exposition can show.

The traditional view. The traditional Christian view of revelation—one still held by many conservative Catholics and Protestants—is that the Bible is the authoritative revelation of God to humanity. (Catholics differ from Protestants in emphasizing the authoritative revelation embodied in the traditional teachings of the church as well.) The Bible is here understood as a source of truth about God, revealing that he exists, what he is like and what he has done in relation to human beings.

The traditional view is often called *the propositional view* because of its emphasis on the Bible as a source of propositional truths. This view is easily caricatured. Not only its enemies have done so; sometimes its friends have caricatured it by taking it to an extreme position. Thus, some have taken the propositional view as the claim that divine revelation consists exclusively of propositions. The Bible has sometimes been seen as a textbook or encyclopedia, a handy source of truth on any field.

Such extreme views must be seen as aberrations, not as the mainstream, traditional position. Christians historically have believed that God has revealed himself in history through his *actions.* He revealed himself to such men as Abraham and Moses by calling them to specific tasks. Later, God spoke through judges and prophets, finally culminating his revelatory actions by actually becoming a human being. Jesus' life, death and resurrection, and the interpretation given of these by the apostles Jesus selected and commissioned, are God's consummating revelatory deeds. All these actions can, of course, be described in propositions, but that does not mean the actions are themselves propositions. The emphasis on the Bible as revelation follows naturally from the belief that the Bible is a divinely inspired record and interpretation of these revelatory actions. Apart from the Bible, human beings would have little knowledge or understanding of God's revelatory actions.

The intent of the propositional view is not, then, to deny that God reveals himself in actions, but to emphasize the fact that one of God's revelatory actions is *speaking* to human beings through divinely inspired, human authors. Nor, of course, is the propositional truth conveyed by the Bible simply presented as a set of facts to be intellectually accepted. The truths include teachings about the human condition, our relation to God and the kind of response to the revelation that God demands. Such truths are properly accepted only when they are acted on.

The special authority of the Bible is often expressed in the claim that it was written by the inspiration of God. Although the authors were human, and their own human characteristics are embodied in the writings, the content of what they wrote was guided by God himself. The writing of the Bible was itself a kind of miracle—a special act of God. The Bible is then, as many Christians put it, "the final authority in matters of faith and practice." Some understand this authority to imply that the Scriptures must be *inerrant* in all matters, including history and science. Others believe that the authority of the Scriptures does not extend to these areas because God did not intend to teach humans in these areas through the Bible. Despite such disagreements, proponents of the traditional view are in agreement that the Bible is itself the Word of God, an authoritative revelation that can be trusted to give us the truth about essential religious matters.

The liberal view. The view of revelation associated with classical liberal theology of the nineteenth century has its sources in two eighteenth-century developments. The first is what is often termed *Enlightenment rationalism.* This philosophical mindset that developed in the eighteenth century emphasized the use of reason to discover truth. The Enlightenment thinkers took reason as contrasting with the blind faith in authority that they believed to be characteristic of the Middle Ages. Kant summarized the spirit of the Enlightenment in a well-known essay in which he claimed that to be truly enlightened is "to dare to use your own reason."[1] The spirit of the Enlightenment was hostile to the claim that a particular historical book could have special authority over the individual. The worldview of the Enlightenment was also not favorable to miracles and other special acts of God. As scientific knowledge of the laws of nature developed, belief in miracles and the like was regarded as superstition.

The second important factor in the development of the classical liberal view of revelation was the growth of *higher criticism.* Biblical scholars began to investigate the Scriptures in the same way that they looked at other classical texts. They put forth historical and literary hypotheses, claiming, for example, that the Pentateuch, instead of being the work of a single, divinely inspired author, reflected the work of many different people over a long period of time. Prophecies which seemed to have been miraculously fulfilled were said to have been written after the fulfilling events. Stories of miracles were regarded as interpolations added by pious commentators at a later date, not eye-witness reports.

How did philosophical rationalism and biblical criticism interact? Clearly, the higher biblical criticism provided much impetus for challenging the traditional view of the Bible as a special, revelatory set of documents. By undermining scriptural authority, it strengthened the position of those who were skeptical of miracles and other special acts of God. However, biblical critics often borrowed philosophical assumptions, which affected their historical-literary conclusions. The two movements reinforced one another, and it is probably not possible to say which caused which.

The upshot of all this is a view of the Bible as a purely human book, a unique record of the evolving religious consciousness of the Jewish people. The Jewish people had unique religious sensitivities; they were a people of religious genius, just as the Greeks were a people of philosophical and artistic genius. Present in the biblical record are the experiences of a people who, beginning from faith in a jealous tribal god, gradually developed faith in a God of love and justice, a God who is a God of all people. This revelation culminates in the profound teachings of Jesus, who is viewed as emphasizing the fatherhood of God and the brotherhood of man.

Thus, on the liberal view, although the Bible may be an especially valuable resource, it is a fully human book, not one with divine authority. We must critically reflect on the Scriptures in the light of reason and experience. Any authority that it possesses is due to its inherent profundity or truthfulness, but these are characteristics that, in the final analysis, we must be able to discern and evaluate ourselves.

The nonpropositional view. The nonpropositional view of revelation can be seen as a kind of compromise between the traditional view and the liberal view. This perspective developed as a twentieth-century reaction to liberalism and is often associated with what is termed *neo-orthodox theology*. However, its proponents claim that the position is consistent with central elements of the theology of the Protestant Reformers Luther and Calvin.

The nonpropositional view emphasizes that God is a personal being and that divine revelation is thus the revealing of a person. God does not reveal propositions for our assent; he reveals *himself*. God's self-revelation consists of his saving actions, which were perceived and interpreted by his faithful people. Like the traditional view, the nonpropositional view holds that God has acted in unique and special ways in history. However, like the liberal view, the Bible is seen as fallible, since it is only a human witness to that revelation. Jesus is said to be the true Word of God; the Bible is a witness to God's revelation but is not itself revelation, except insofar as God continues to confront human beings through its teachings. God is still a God who encounters his people; thus, when the Bible is properly proclaimed, it may become the Word of God.

Is the Traditional View Defensible?

If it is not reasonable to believe that God can and does intervene in the natural order, then both the traditional and the nonpropositional views of revelation are unacceptable. Both involve the idea of God's performing special revelatory actions. If God does not perform special actions, or if humans cannot recognize such actions, then the liberal view of revelation is the only alternative consistent with religious belief.

The liberal view, in effect, reduces special revelation to natural revelation. What were formerly called special revelations are simply especially valuable instances of the general knowledge of God made possible by the religious dimension of general experience. While this position may ultimately turn out to be the only one possible for a theist, it would seem a mistake to adopt it without considering whether it is reasonable to believe in special acts of God. If God does perform special revelatory acts, this would be a significant source of information about him. It would be a great disadvantage to be limited to general revelation. It therefore is worthwhile to see what can be said on behalf of the traditional and nonpropositional views. Special revelation should not be abandoned unless it is necessary to do so.

Both the traditional and nonpropositional views involve the philosophical embarrassment (if it is such) of belief in "special acts" of God that are miraculous or quasi-miraculous in character. Philosophically, it is hard to argue for one view or the other. A few points can be made, however, on behalf of the traditional view.

First, it would be a good thing for theology if the traditional view were correct. The task of theology is to gain a true understanding of God and his dealings with us. If God has acted specially in history to give us such an understanding, that is certainly significant. Hence it is clearly more desirable, theologically, that the nonpropositional view be correct than the liberal view. But for similar reasons, it would be even better if the traditional view were correct. For if God not only has acted in history, but also has disclosed the meaning of those actions, our knowledge of God would be greatly enriched. So it is reasonable not to abandon the traditional view unless one has good reason to do so. It at least deserves serious consideration.

Second, *speaking* is itself a kind of action. If God is a God capable of special actions at all, there is no a priori reason for thinking that speaking to (or through) human beings would not be in his repertoire of actions. If God does speak to or through human beings, his address must have *content*. One cannot simply speak; one must say something. Thus, the propositions expressed when God speaks to (or through) any person count as revealed truths.

Third, many arguments given against the traditional view presuppose false dichotomies. The traditional view is identified with one of its elements, which is then regarded as a mutually exclusive alternative to some other element. A false disjunction is created. For example, it is sometimes urged that what God reveals is not propositions but rather himself as a personal reality. "*Either* God reveals himself *or* he reveals propositions." Now it is certainly true that a personal God is not a set of propositions and that an encounter with a personal God is not reducible to the acquisition of propositional knowledge. It would be a mistake, however, to conclude from this that propositional revelation and personal encounter are mutually exclusive. Getting to know someone is not reducible to getting to know things about someone, but it certainly may include the latter. In fact, it is plausible to claim that the former process must include or presuppose some of the latter. It is difficult to imagine knowing a person and at the same time knowing nothing about that person.

In a similar way, it is sometimes urged that the traditional view leads to an inadequate view of faith. It is urged that faith, on the traditional view, is simply intellectual acceptance of propositional truth, while true faith is a personal response to God in trust and commitment. "*Either* faith is intellectual assent *or* it is personal trust." Here, two responses can be made. First, the criticism foists a caricature on the traditional view of faith. Almost every Christian theologian has affirmed that saving faith is more than intellectual assent. Second, a false disjunction is again being presented. It must be granted that personal faith is *more* than cognitive assent to doctrine, but it certainly can include such assent. Once more, in fact, it can be argued that it must do so. If I believe *in* (trust) a certain person—say, a political leader—I must also believe some things *about* him.

Proponents of the traditional view can acknowledge that the nonpropositional view is a valuable corrective to what has sometimes been a misplaced emphasis in the traditional view. It should be recognized that God's revelation consists of his activity, in which he reveals himself, and that the human response to this revelation must include the involvement of the whole person. But there are no good philosophical reasons for thinking that such a revelation precludes God's giving humans certain propositional truths to be believed; in fact, there are good reasons for thinking such a revelation would include the communication of propositional content. There is also no good reason to think that personal trust in God somehow rules out belief in that content.

None of this implies that God *has* revealed himself in the way the traditional view supposes. It simply implies that if God reveals himself at all, one could expect the revelation to consist of the kind of thing the traditional view accepts. There are no particular philosophical difficulties present in the traditional view that are avoided by the nonpropositional view.

A further difficulty with the nonpropositional view is the problem of distinguishing the "revelatory events" from the verbal record and interpretation of those events. Logically, of course, an event is certainly distinct from a written record and interpretation of the event. But the particular "saving events" which the nonpropositional view regards as revelation cannot be known independently of the verbal records we have of these, whether written or oral tradition. Since we have no access to the events other than through the verbal accounts, and the Scriptural revelations constitute by far the most important part of such accounts, it is hard to see how one can separate the event from its interpretation, at least from our perspective.

The crucial philosophical question seems to be whether God can and does perform special acts. If he does, then no special philosophical difficulties will be raised by holding to the traditional view. We shall turn our attention then to the question of whether it is reasonable to believe that God performs (or has performed) such actions.

What Is a Miracle?

A special act of God, as we are considering it, can be understood as an act that God performs at a particular place and time, an act distinct from his "normal" activity of sustaining the universe, including its natural processes. To an observer, such an act would appear as an intervention from "outside" the system. However, this is a slightly misleading way of describing such an action, since God, as the sustainer of all things, is always involved with and "inside" his creation. Nevertheless, this description of a special act of God closely parallels one traditional definition of a miracle.

In his famous essay "Of Miracles," Hume defines a miracle as a "*transgression of a law of nature by a particular volition of the Deity, or by the interposition of some invisible agent.*"[2] Here Hume sensibly leaves open the possibility that a miracle could be performed by any supernatural agent—angels or demons, for example. While the possibility of such miracles is important, we are mainly interested in divine miracles, so in the following discussion, we will for the most part consider a miracle as a special act of God.

It might appear that there could be special acts of God that would not be "transgressions of laws of nature," so that miracles, on Hume's definition, would be merely one type of special act of God. On reflection, however, it seems evident that any special act of God would be an exception to ordinary natural processes, simply in virtue of its qualifying as *special*, though it would not have to deviate obviously from ordinary patterns. If the laws of nature are taken to be descriptions of God's normal creative activity, then any special acts would necessarily differ in some way from those natural processes.

Hume's definition of a miracle is often attacked on a variety of grounds. Sometimes, the objection is made that miracles are not really violations or transgressions of natural laws. Since these laws are descriptive, rather than prescriptive, it is misleading to describe God's action in deviating from them, on occasion, as a violation of a law. A useful point is being made here, and some people are no doubt misled by the connotations of the words "law" and "violation." However, what many philosophers (including perhaps Hume himself) mean by a violation of a natural law is simply an exception to the *normal* processes of nature. This is quite consistent with a descriptive understanding of natural laws.

Another objection to the Humean definition argues that miracles are not really exceptions to the laws of nature. Natural laws describe what will occur, given a particular set of initial conditions. When those conditions do not hold, the law is not applicable. When a miracle occurs, however, the initial conditions will necessarily be different, since God's special activity will be part of those conditions. Therefore, the law has not really been violated.

It is certainly true that something different happens when a miracle occurs. When God steps in "specially," a new factor is added to the situation. But there is no reason to think that the advocates of the Humean definition are ignorant of this fact. The assumption which lies behind this definition is that there are regular processes which bring about results in the natural order. Assuming these processes are divine in origin, they represent God's "constant" activity. When God "steps in" in some special way, his activity is, by definition, exceptional in nature, and it is in one sense natural that the effects of God's activity should be exceptional as well. Since God has acted specially, the effects will be somewhat special. No laws are violated in the sense that something irrational has occurred. Still, the events in question will be *different* from the normal course of nature. There is no apparent reason then to quarrel with the definition of a miracle as an exception to the laws of nature that is brought about by a special act of God.

Some theologians, usually those who have already given up belief in miracles in the traditional sense, object to the Humean definition on the grounds that it misses what is really important about a miracle. On this view, miracles are revelatory events—*signs*—and not supernaturally caused exceptions to the usual course of nature. To this it must be responded that in Christianity and other major religions the most important function of miracles is indeed that of being signs, events that witness to God's power and character and attest to the authority of prophets and apostles. However, at least normally, the astounding supernatural quality of the miracles is partly what makes them signs and revelatory events. People in biblical times were quite aware that a human being does not, in the normal course of nature, rise from the dead or become pregnant while still a virgin. Such "unnatural" events were therefore seen as evidence that God was at work in a special way.

It is possible, of course, for events to function as signs without being miracles in the Humean sense. We have already, in our chapter on religious experience, discussed how an awareness of God might be mediated through the natural order. If anyone wishes to use the term "miracle" for the broad class of revelatory events or experiences, he is free to do so. In that case, "miracles" in the Humean sense would be a species of the broader class of miracles. We see no reason to adopt this terminology, however, since the word "sign" can be employed for the broader category of revelatory events.

It is not necessary, of course, that a special act of God always produce an obvious exception to the laws of nature. Suppose, for example, that a crucial bolt on an airliner is about to fail, and that, in response to prayers for the safekeeping of those on board, God miraculously fuses the bolt. To all outward appearances, the flight is uneventful; nevertheless, the safe arrival of the plane is a miracle. Such a miracle would be hard to detect and thus would lack some of the features of miracles that function as signs. On our definition such an act on God's part would still qualify as a miracle. Such a possibility provides another reason for not identifying miracles with signs. Obviously, the miracles of a religion such as Christianity are not simply bizarre events or stunts. They have a function and a purpose, and usually that function is a revelatory one. But it seems possible for there to be signs that are not strictly miracles, and miracles which are not strictly signs.

Is It Reasonable to Believe in Miracles?

Hume, after giving his famous definition of miracles, gives an equally famous argument against believing in their occurrence. Actually, Hume gives two distinct types of arguments in his essay. The first is an a priori argument designed to show that no ordinary evidence would ever suffice to make belief in a miracle reasonable. The second argument attempts to show that the actual evidence put forward on behalf of miracles is pretty weak. We will consider these two arguments separately. Both of the arguments are epistemological in character: that is, Hume does not attempt to prove that miracles are impossible but rather to show that we do not or could not have sufficient evidence to be justified in believing that any miracles have actually occurred.

It is perhaps worth pausing to consider why Hume does not attempt to show, in a straightforward way, that miracles do not or could not occur. After all, it is sometimes claimed that miracles are out-and-out impossible. It is sometimes further alleged that science has somehow *shown* the impossibility of miracles. Even sophisticated philosophers sometimes make such claims.[3] Hume does not, however, and it is easy to see why he does not. Whether there is a God—and, if so, whether he performs any special actions—would seem to be, in Hume's terminology, "matters of fact." Hume argues strenuously that whenever we deal with matters of fact, questions of truth must be decided on the basis of experience. We cannot say a priori what kinds of beings there are or how these beings behave. Hume is surely right here, and it would be foolish of him to contradict his own principle by claiming to know a priori that miracles never occur.

Sometimes it is alleged that miracles are impossible because they are violations of laws of nature. The underlying assumption behind this objection is that the laws of nature are *necessary*. As we have seen, in one sense miracles are indeed violations of laws of nature, but the laws of nature are most plausibly interpreted as descriptive of the actual processes of nature, not as descriptions of the way nature *had to be*.[4] (As we discussed in our treatment of the fine-tuning argument, physicists can actually calculate what the world would have been like, in certain limited respects, had the laws of nature been somewhat different.) The laws of nature are contingent, it seems, not necessary. Thus, whether the uniformities of nature are absolute or admit of exceptions would seem to be, once again, a matter of fact that cannot be decided a priori.

Countering Hume's first argument. Let us now examine Hume's first, general argument. This argument presupposes certain conceptions of probability and evidence. In his argument Hume assumes that the individual considering his argument has had no firsthand experience of miracles but is forced to rely on testimony. In all cases of testimony, one can distinguish between the credibility of the witness and the intrinsic probability of the content of the testimony. Extremely unlikely stories require numerous, trustworthy witnesses. Extremely likely stories may be rationally accepted even on the basis of flimsy witnesses.

What is the intrinsic probability of a miracle? According to Hume it is extremely low—as low as one could imagine. The probability of an event, he says, is determined by the frequency with which it has been observed to occur. A miracle, as an exception to the laws of nature, must then be the least likely event possible. Hume writes, "A miracle is a violation of the laws of nature; and as a firm and unalterable experience has established these laws, the proof against a miracle, from the very nature of the fact, is as entire as any argument from experience can possibly be imagined."[5]

We will leave aside the question-begging reference to experience as "unalterable," which would contradict Hume's own view of experience. Hume is claiming, in effect, that miracles are by definition so improbable that even the most impressive testimony would merely balance the counterevidence provided by the improbability of the miracle. Only testimony so strong that its falsehood would itself be more miraculous than the alleged miracle would suffice to rationally convince one of a miracle.[6]

Hume's argument here seems open to criticism on several counts. First, he does not give adequate consideration to the possibility of firsthand observation of a miracle, which would circumvent the problems raised by testimony (although, of course, other problems could be raised about the reliability of the experience itself). Second, he does not consider the kinds of physical effects or traces that a miracle might leave, which might provide evidence for its occurrence independent of testimony. A healed withered leg stands as evidence of a miraculous event, apart from the testimony of the one healed. The most serious defect, however, seems to lie in the view of probability that underlies Hume's account.

Hume's view presupposes that the probability of the occurrence of a certain type of event is straightforwardly determined by the frequency with which events of that type occur.[7] This, however, is surely much too wooden and simple a view, as evidenced by the fact that were it universally accepted, it would create enormous difficulties for the historian, who deals with unique and unrepeatable events all the time. We might take, as an example, the collision of a planet and a comet. Events of this type, if they occur at all, are no doubt infrequent and therefore improbable, on Hume's view. However, though at any given moment such a collision may be improbable, it does not follow from this that it is improbable that such events have ever occurred or will ever occur. In a similar way a believer in miracles might agree that at any given moment the occurrence of a miracle is improbable, since miracles are unusual events, but she could still claim that the occurrence of miracles *at some time or other* is far from improbable.

Furthermore, even an unusual event, such as the collision of a comet and a planet, may be highly probable at a given moment. If we know the velocities and orbits of a certain planet and comet, their collision at a certain time may be nearly certain. In this instance we estimate probability on the basis of our knowledge of the actual characteristics of the heavenly bodies, and we do not limit ourselves to our knowledge of the frequency of such events in the past. In a similar way the defender of miracles may claim that whether miracles occur depends largely on whether God exists, what kind of God he is and what purposes he has. Given enough knowledge of God and his purposes in relation to human history, the occurrence of a miracle might be, in some situations, highly probable or at least not nearly so improbable as Hume suggests. This is one point where natural theology might make a substantive contribution to religious knowledge. If strong reasons can be given for belief in a personal God, then it might be rash to give too low an estimate of the general probability of a miracle.

Even in the absence of any firm knowledge about God and his purposes, however, it still would be rash to claim, with Hume, that the probability of a miracle is vanishingly small. Rather, it would appear more reasonable to conclude, in this case, that it is hard, if not impossible, to estimate the a priori probability of a miracle, in which case, one should try to look at the evidence for miracles with a somewhat open, though cautiously skeptical, mind.

Countering Hume's second argument. At this point Hume's second type of argument against miracles becomes relevant. Here, Hume claims that, as a matter of fact, the evidence adduced in favor of miracles is pretty weak. Hume points out that the testimony in favor of miracles usually comes from uneducated people who lived in far-off places and times, in "ignorant and barbarous nations."[8] He notes the many forged and false stories of miracles and the human tendency to believe in the exotic and strange, which undermines the credibility of such stories.[9] Also, Hume claims that the miracles that function as evidence for one religion function as counterevidence for the miracles of other religions.[10]

These specific criticisms are, to some extent, judgments that must be evaluated by the historian, rather than the philosopher, and the correctness of such claims must be considered on a case-by-case basis. Certainly, not all alleged miracles are equally well attested, and Hume is probably right with respect to the great majority of purported miracles. But it is not at all obvious that his criticisms are powerful against *all* alleged miracles.

Some of Hume's criticisms seem to presuppose an overly arrogant attitude toward non-Western and "premodern" cultures. In biblical times, for example, contemporary scientific knowledge was obviously lacking, but people knew, just as certainly as people do today, that in the normal course of nature it is not possible for a child to be born of a virgin or for a man to rise from the dead.[11] Hume also seems mistaken in assuming that miracles from one religion automatically constitute counterevidence for the miracles of other religions. Even if Hume were right here, it would not follow that the evidence for all miracles would be invalidated, for the evidence for the miracles of one religion might be much more impressive than the evidence for the miracles of another. It should also be recognized that the "love of the marvelous" that Hume cites is balanced in many people by an equally strong skepticism. In general, there seems to be no substitute for careful consideration of specific miracle claims on their own merits.

Contemporary arguments. Some contemporary philosophers have attempted to rule out miracles through a different argument. On their view, the laws of nature are defined as descriptions of what happens *always* or *universally.* If an exception to a law of nature occurs, this only shows that the supposed law of nature in question is not a genuine law of nature, since it did not hold universally. If we knew the true laws of nature, the apparent exception would be seen to be fully natural.[12]

However, in the absence of a priori knowledge of the laws of nature—which, obviously, we do not and cannot have—it is difficult to see how this critic could possibly know that there are laws of nature which would account for the alleged miraculous events. There may not be any laws which hold universally, in the strictest sense, if God occasionally acts in a special manner. This might seem to create a problem for the defender of miracles. How can he define a miracle as an exception to the laws of nature if there are no such laws? This is not a genuine problem, however. Even if the defender of miracles gives the term "law" to the critic, he can develop a similar concept to describe natural uniformities that always hold *except* when God (or some other supernatural power) operates in a special manner. A "miracle" can then be defined as an exception to these normal uniformities, which hold generally but not universally.

A second type of contemporary challenge is found in the writings of Patrick Nowell-Smith, who argues that to call an event a miracle is to attempt to explain the event, to view it as an effect of God's action. Nowell-Smith claims that a true explanation of an event always involves a reference to a natural law. Since miracles, however, are exceptions to natural laws, and there do not seem to be any relevant laws which describe the behavior of God, then no real explanation has been given.[13]

Nowell-Smith's claim that all explanation requires a reference to laws of nature seems false, however. Historical explanations, as well as explanations of human action generally, are often accepted which involve no reference to any known laws of nature. We explain an act as the doing of a person who had certain purposes and intentions, without knowledge of any natural laws describing what always happens in such a situation. Such laws may exist, but we neither rely on them nor need to know about them to give an explanation of the action. Since theists conceive of God as a person, this kind of "personal explanation" provides an obvious analogy to the form of explanation that is implicit in calling an event a miracle.

This analogy provides a basis for recognizing the kind of evidence needed to regard an event as a miracle. The case for regarding some historical event as the work of some particular historical figure depends on the evidence we have for the nature of the event, as well as on our knowledge of the character and intentions of the person in question. Particularly important is our ability to place the alleged action in the context of the person's life. In a similar way, the religious believer's case for a miracle will depend on such factors as (1) our knowledge of the event (that is, do we have good reason to suppose it is a violation of a law of nature?), (2) our knowledge of God's character and purposes, and (3) our knowledge of God's other actions. By and large, the alleged miracles of most religions, especially Christianity, are not random, isolated occurrences, but rather events that are part of a meaningful context, the story of God's redemptive activity.

Richard Swinburne has developed the concept of a "non-repeatable counter-instance to a law of nature" to describe a miracle.[14] When an event occurs which appears to contravene a law of nature, two options are possible. We can regard the event as evidence for the falsity of the law, or we can regard it as an exception to a law that otherwise holds. The former is reasonable when there is evidence that the exception is repeatable. This means that if the natural situation were reduplicated, the exception would occur again. In such a case we would probably look for some more fundamental law to explain the deviation. If, however, the exception seems to be a nonrepeatable occurrence, then it would seem irrational to abandon belief in a law of nature that holds in every other case. The apparent exception would be an exception to a genuine law of nature. (There is no compelling reason to use the phrase “law of nature” only to describe laws that hold without exception.)

In certain situations it would appear plausible to regard such nonrepeatable counterinstances as miracles. Suppose that one had good reason to believe in God and good reason to believe that he sometimes answers prayer. At the very moment that one individual is praying to God for the restoration of the limb of an amputee, a new limb suddenly appears in full view of witnesses. It is hard to see how one could avoid concluding that a miracle had occurred in such a setting.

It seems rash, therefore, for philosophers or others to claim dogmatically that miracles cannot happen. Miracles seem possible at least, and it also seems possible for there to be compelling evidence for their occurrence—evidence of the ordinary historical kind. The degree of evidence necessary to have a good basis for belief in a miracle is difficult to determine, however. One’s judgment here will be heavily shaped by one’s view of the likelihood of God’s existence and one’s view of God’s nature and purposes. It seems at least possible, however, that a reasonable person could become convinced that miracles have occurred, even if he did not have a previously high estimate of the likelihood of God’s existence, so long as he were not firmly convinced that God’s existence is impossible. Indeed, it seems reasonable that God might reveal much about his character and purposes through miracles. He might show that he is a miracle-working kind of God by performing some miracles.

Can a Revelation Have Special Authority?

We can now return to the question of whether a special revelation, understood in the traditional sense, is possible. If special revelation is best viewed as a special act of God whereby God confronts human beings and reveals himself to them, then the question, at bottom, depends on the question of whether miracles are possible. It does seem possible for miracles to occur, and the type of miracle required for special revelation appears to present no new difficulties. Such a revelation would therefore seem to be possible, and judgments as to whether such a revelation has actually occurred should be made in the same way as judgments as to whether other particular miracles have occurred.

One special challenge does present itself, however. If God were to inspire a human being to write a book or utter some word of exhortation, it would not necessarily be obvious that a miracle had occurred. Such a miracle would be, in some ways, like the hypothetical case of the airliner discussed earlier (see p. 128). It might appear to observers that a perfectly natural explanation of the author's "inspiration" could be given. Probably, it is for this reason that claimants to revelation, such as the Old Testament prophets or Jesus, are alleged to have performed other, more obvious miracles. The obvious miracles have the function of certifying or authenticating the individual's claim to have the unique authority that is possessed by those who are recipients of special inspiration.

Could a reasonable person attribute special authority to any particular religious revelation? Often, philosophers have insinuated that the acceptance of such an authority would spell the end of rationality. It is frequently claimed that an individual must choose between revelation and reason, or between authority and reason. As we have viewed revelation, however, it is simply a special class of experiences made possible by God's action. The question of whether some special revelation could reasonably be regarded as having special authority is simply the question of whether certain experiences of certain people could have a special authority in the construction of reasonable beliefs.

All persons recognize the limitations of their own knowledge and experience, and the reasonableness of relying on the authority of someone more knowledgeable. Why should this not be the case with respect to religious knowledge as well? Were any individual to have a special revelatory experience of God, that individual certainly would seem to be in a position of having some knowledge of God which exceeds that of people who have not had such experiences. Were one in a position to know that they had had such an experience, it would be reasonable to regard their testimony as having special authority. Of course, ultimately the authority of the prophet or bearer of the revelation derives from the authority of the God who is the source of the revelation. Since God, if he exists, is omniscient, it is hardly irrational to believe what God says, assuming one has reason to believe that it is indeed God who speaks.

The question, of course, is whether one could ever be in a position to know that someone else had truly had an experience of receiving special revelation from God. Here again is where the importance of "authenticating miracles" appears. Perhaps it is the case that when God issues some special revelation to a particular individual which he intends for others as well, he also commands that individual to testify to what has been revealed and authenticates the individual's testimony by way of performing some miracle which serves as obvious evidence of a divine "stamp of approval" on the individual's message. There seems to be scriptural evidence in both the Old and New Testaments that this is the method which God typically—if not always—employs. Those who witness the miracles are thus provided evidence of the divine authority by which the "messenger" speaks, rather than being asked to simply take it on the messenger's word.

Revelation and reason then are not necessarily rival methods of knowing, because it is possible to accept a revelation in a reasonable manner. It is also possible, of course, to accept one in an unreasonable manner. A reasonable person should not regard a revelation as a substitute for thought and reflection, but if he is truly thoughtful and reflective, he will also see that it is not reasonable to rule out the possibility of a revelation on a dogmatic, a priori basis.

6

Religion, Modernity and Science

In the present intellectual and cultural milieu, we find a number of different critiques of religion and religious belief, not all of them consistent with one another. One line of argument contends that religious belief is no longer feasible for reflective, educated people; another laments that religious belief continues to hold such prominence in so many peoples' lives and attributes various social ills to its continued existence. Some allege that religion has been disproved—by science or sociology or philosophy or something else, perhaps—while others allege that religion does not even enjoy the dignity of making meaningful claims which could be disproved.[1] In this and the following chapter, we will address some of the more prominent critiques, beginning with those that have their roots in the natural and social sciences.

Modernity and Religious Belief

Many writers approach the question of religious belief today in a thoroughly sociological manner. In the twentieth century there was a widespread conviction that a trend toward secularization inevitably goes hand in hand with the development of a modern, industrialized society. Accordingly, there was much talk about whether it was possible for "modern man" to believe in God or other supernatural beings in the traditional sense. Theologian Rudolf Bultmann (1884-1976) went so far as to claim, "It is impossible to use electric light and the wireless and to avail ourselves of modern medical and surgical discoveries, and at the same time to believe in the New Testament world of spirits and miracles."[2] Others, such as death-of-God theologian Thomas J. J. Altizer or Bishop John Robinson, extended Bultmann's perspective on "spirits and miracles" to the very idea of God as a distinct person. These developments raised for religious belief what may be termed "the problem of modernity."

Since the heyday of these writers, religious belief has, in certain parts of the world, remained strong or even enjoyed some kind of resurgence. Nevertheless, despite any such recent, localized gains, there continues to be an overall decline in the percentage of religious believers in Western industrialized countries, at least among intellectuals, and particularly in Western Europe. Thus, the basic challenge of modernity remains: does religious belief remain a "live option"—to use the language of William James—for educated, reflective, intellectually honest people today?

If it is correct that religious belief has declined overall among educated people in recent times, this is an interesting fact and no doubt worth some reflection. Many explanations of such a fact are possible, especially given the emotional nature of religious faith and its implications for one's personal life. It would be extremely rash to conclude from such a fact that religious belief is necessarily irrational. And such a sociological fact must be balanced by other interesting sociological facts, such as the amazing persistence of religious faith in China and the former Soviet Union during periods in which there were repeated attempts by totalitarian governments to extinguish it, as well as the fact that a much higher percentage of Americans are church members today than in the era of the Revolutionary War.

In general, deciding the reasonableness of belief in God on the basis of sociological facts is like deciding whom to vote for in an election on the basis of who is leading in the public opinion polls.

In both cases, one has abdicated one's personal responsibility to ascertain what is true or best in favor of the anonymous authority of what existential writers like to call "the crowd." Certainly, historians and sociologists should continue to explore modernity and its causes and implications, but it is a mistake to think that such studies will answer such basic human questions as whether God exists. Indeed, in the current climate it would seem to be a good thing if theologians and others would cease to utter judgments about what modern human beings *can* believe and instead think more deeply about what they (themselves included) *should* believe. Such sociological pronouncements are a distraction from the pressing task of examining the serious objections to religious belief that have been made.

This brings us back to Bultmann, whose theological influence is still very much felt today. His statement that it is *impossible* to use electric lights and believe in spirits and miracles is, no doubt, a wild exaggeration. Many sophisticated people do continue to believe in spirits and miracles. Some of these believers are scientists and physicians; some are even philosophers. But perhaps Bultmann's real point is not a psychological or sociological claim about what it is possible or impossible to believe, but rather a claim that certain features of the modern world, particularly scientific knowledge, make traditional religious belief irrational. If so, the arguments which try to advance this conclusion should be put on the table for rational examination. Glib generalizations about how scientific knowledge is incompatible with religious faith will not do. If scientific knowledge in some way undermines the reasonableness of religious belief, then certainly it is important for us to know this: the specific features of science that count as objections must be explained, and it must be shown just *how* these features make religious belief untenable. Shortly, we will examine some arguments that purport to do this. But first, we should say a word about the general worldview that takes religious claims to be both false and incompatible with contemporary scientific knowledge.

Naturalism

Naturalism actually comes in various forms, and it is important, for the present discussion, to distinguish these. The view that we have been calling "naturalism" up to this point is more accurately termed *philosophical naturalism:* the view that the only things that exist are "natural" entities—that is, whatever entities are posited by the natural sciences in constructing theories which attempt to explain the natural world. The success of the natural sciences has undoubtedly encouraged the view that nature exists "on its own" and that nothing beyond a scientific explanation is necessary. Whether the philosophical naturalist is right is a question that can be put aside here.[3] (The issue depends, for one thing, on whether it is reasonable to look for an explanation of the contingency of the universe and its beneficial order. These issues were discussed in connection with the cosmological and teleological arguments, and the reader who is interested in pursuing them further should refer back to chapter three.) For present purposes what is important to see is that philosophical naturalism is essentially just the view that there are no supernatural entities: no God, no angels, no immaterial souls or the like. As such, philosophical naturalism cannot itself possibly refute theism because it is simply a denial of theism (and of any other view that posits supernatural entities). To claim that theism is false *because* naturalism is true would be gross question-begging. Furthermore, philosophical naturalism is in no way entailed by any credible scientific theory, nor by the sum total of all such theories. It is, as the name implies, a purely philosophical view, not a view that could enjoy empirical support. Thus, while theism is certainly incompatible with philosophical naturalism, this fact in no way proves that theism is incompatible with science.

A more interesting question is whether theism is incompatible with *methodological naturalism*, and whether methodological naturalism is a presupposition of science. Methodological naturalism is the view that all scientific explanations, as such, must refer only to natural entities and their properties—in short, that an explanation qualifies as "scientific" only if it restricts itself to the natural world. Whether science requires methodological naturalism is controversial.[4] This issue, for example, underlies the debate about whether any theory of the order of the universe that references intelligent design could, in principle, qualify as a scientific view. Those who say yes reject methodological naturalism in favor of a view in which science is simply the search for true explanations of natural phenomena, without any further restrictions as to what kinds of explanations can qualify as "scientific."

Even if science *does* include a commitment to methodological naturalism, however, it seems clear that this in no way proves that theism is incompatible with science, much less that theism is false. If science is limited to naturalistic explanations of natural phenomena, this implies simply that science could be "blind" to certain truths; some features of the world may be, in principle, impossible for science to even recognize, much less explain. This will be the case if there are in fact any "nonnatural" entities. Thus, methodological naturalism neither refutes theism nor is incompatible with theism. If methodological naturalism is accepted, all that follows is that science does not have a corner on truth—unless, perhaps, philosophical naturalism also turns out to be true (which, as we have seen, cannot possibly be proven one way or the other by science). One can affirm, consistently, both methodological naturalism and theism; if one does so, one will take science to explain a certain part of the world (the natural realm) and theism to explain a different part (the supernatural realm).

It seems then that naturalism in its various forms cannot provide the basis of a refutation of theism, nor can it demonstrate that religion and science are incompatible. If any such incompatibility exists, it must be found in the scientific theories themselves. Thus, we return now to the question of whether developments in modern science do, in fact, provide any kind of rational impediment to religious belief, such that educated people today must make a choice between the two.

Do the Natural Sciences Undermine Religious Belief?

In examining the difficulties the sciences allegedly pose for religious belief, it is helpful to distinguish problems stemming from the natural sciences from those stemming from the social sciences. The idea that the development and growth of the natural sciences constitutes a difficulty for the religious believer is rather widespread, despite the fact that many of the greatest natural scientists believe in God. What exactly are these difficulties supposed to be?

Some are hardly worth considering. For example, some purport to find a problem in the vastness of the universe and in the relative spatial insignificance of the earth. It is hasty, at best, to estimate spiritual significance purely on the basis of physical size. The earth may turn out to be a pretty important place when all is said and done. In any case, since most religious believers regard God as the Creator of the whole universe, the immensity of that universe can only add to our impression of the Creator's greatness. It is perfectly consistent with theism to believe that God may have created other beings in other parts of the universe, and for all we know God may be just as concerned with such beings as we on earth think he is with us.

Such issues raise an important distinction, however. The question of whether the natural sciences *in general* undermine religious belief must be distinguished from the question of whether there are *particular* tenets of science that are at odds with *particular* tenets of theism. The issues just discussed fall into the latter category, and none of these poses a serious challenge for religious belief.

A somewhat more troubling idea—one that falls under the discussion of possible "general" clashes—is the idea that the success of the natural sciences in producing *explanations* of the universe (or parts of it, anyway) has somehow proven the "God hypothesis" superfluous or even false. On this view, theology and science are competing theories which each try to explain natural events. This is the view of evolutionary biologist Richard Dawkins, who claims,

> More generally it is completely unrealistic to claim, as [scientist Stephen Jay] Gould and many others do, that religion keeps itself away from science's turf, restricting itself to morals and values. A universe with a supernatural presence would be a fundamentally and qualitatively different kind of universe from one without. The difference is, inescapably, a scientific difference. Religions make existence claims, and this means scientific claims.[5]

On Dawkins view, religion and science cannot be reconciled as "nonoverlapping magisteria," as Gould and others have suggested,[6] because religion and science make competing and incompatible claims: both are in the business of explaining what the world is really like. The success of the natural sciences, however, gives it the upper hand, and thus scientific explanations "crowd out" theological explanations, on Dawkins's view.

An idea similar to this is prominent in nineteenth-century philosopher and sociologist Auguste Comte's description of the history of science. On Comte's view it is characteristic of a primitive society to give theological explanations of phenomena: "It thunders because Thor throws his hammer." As science matures, such explanations are replaced by mechanistic ones involving natural regularities.

Both Dawkins's and Comte's views are open to challenge on several counts. Dawkins, for one, is surely right that God's existence would make a fundamental and qualitative difference in the world. But Dawkins further suggests, in the aforementioned passage, that every existence claim falls under the purview of science—to claim for any X that X exists is to make a scientific claim—which hardly seems plausible. "There is a prime number between 1 and 3" is (arguably) an existence claim, and yet it clearly is not a scientific claim. This response might strike one as rather glib, like a lawyer's trying to get his client off on a technicality, but in fact, the point is quite serious. Wherever existence claims are made that involve matters of metaphysics, we should not expect the entities in question to be scientifically verifiable; otherwise, the issue would not be a metaphysical one. Whatever evidence there might be for these entities must be *rational* evidence—evidence provided, for example, by philosophical arguments. The existence of numbers is a metaphysical issue, and—in the context of a challenge like Dawkins's—so is the existence of God and other "religious" entities (immaterial souls, for example). Clearly, then, not all existence claims are scientific claims.

Perhaps Dawkins's point, however, is simply that, were God to exist, his existence—and activity, presumably—would have scientifically observable *effects* in the world. But on this point the theist need not disagree, so long as "scientifically observable" is not construed in a way that begs the question in favor of philosophical naturalism. The theist can point, for example, to the fine-tuning of the universe as one such effect of God's activity. Miracles also are effects of God's activity in the world, and they are disqualified as "scientifically observable" only if the term is stipulated to denote something like "capable of being repeated in the lab" rather than "capable of being empirically observed by one or more persons on some occasion." Dawkins cannot, without loading the dice against theism, insist *both* that God's existence must have scientifically observable effects *and* that "scientifically observable" be defined in a way that ensures all the evidence of God's existence is ruled out.

Comte, on the other hand, has apparently confused theology with mythology. Thor's hammer seems to be an instance of the latter, and there are great differences between such mythology and the theology of the great world religions. For another, Comte fails to see that *magic* would be a better candidate as the historical ancestor of modern science than either mythology or theology.

The most serious objection to Comte, however, is that he misconstrues the nature of a theological explanation. This, in fact, is a mistake committed by Comte and Dawkins alike. Though believers have sometimes understood God's activity as an immediate explanation for natural phenomena (particularly in the case of miracles), it does not appear that religion and science usually give competing explanations, on the same level, for ordinary events. Natural science pushes further and further in its explanatory quest, but any claim that its explanations are ultimate and final seems not to be a testable, scientific claim. Science tries to describe the structures and processes of nature. The question as to whether there is anything more ultimate than nature, which explains nature itself, with its processes and structures, is one that cannot be answered by science itself—which is not to say that scientific knowledge is always irrelevant in answering such a question.

Theology, on the other hand, is not (or need not be) interested directly in the processes of nature—though it may well be interested in the implications of some of these processes. Theology sees the laws of nature as descriptions of the orderly processes that God instituted and maintains. Theology tries to answer the question of why nature exists at all, and why nature has the orderly characteristics that science investigates. Science and theology do not, therefore, seem to be essential rivals, because the explanations they offer are not of the same type or on the same level. Science tries to tell us what goes on and how it goes on. Theology tries to tell us why the whole thing goes on and who stands behind it. It seems, then, that something like Gould's notion of "nonoverlapping magisteria" could be right after all.

We thus conclude that science and religion do not—or at least need not—conflict *in general*. However, this is not to say that *particular* theological doctrines could not conflict with *particular* scientific theories. For example, the steady-state cosmological theory, though compatible with theism in general, would appear to conflict with the views of many Christians that the universe had a beginning. (For this reason, many Christians are happy that the big bang theory currently enjoys more scientific support.) Thus, clashes between science and religion continue to be real possibilities, just as they have been in the past. These conflicts should not lead the reflective theist to automatically conclude that her religious beliefs are false, much less irrational, but it should motivate her to explore the relevant scientific, philosophical and theological issues further, until some satisfactory solution has been reached. It is surely a mistake to regard *either* prevailing scientific theories *or* one's preferred theological system as automatically "trumping" the other, without need for further, careful consideration.

Objections from the Social Sciences

In the nineteenth and twentieth centuries some of the sharpest objections to religious belief emerged not from the natural sciences but from the social sciences. Although challenges were posed in a number of areas, probably the most significant came from psychologist Sigmund Freud and sociologists Émile Durkheim and Karl Marx. We shall look at the sociologists first, and then turn to psychology.

Challenges from sociology. Many sociologists view the gods or God as a product of what one might term "the collective imagination of a society." God is, on this view, a "projection," not a real being. He is created by society for social purposes, such as gaining greater control over individuals. Sociologists often see belief in God as providing a focal point for the shared values of a society, particularly those values considered holy.

The particular forms of a sociological theory of religion, of course, reflect the characteristics of particular forms of sociological theory. French sociologist Émile Durkheim stressed the way in which religious belief contributes to the cohesion and harmonious functioning of a society. Karl Marx, on the other hand, seeing society as permeated by conflict and strife, viewed religious belief as related to class conflict. Marx is well known for his claim that religion is the "opium of the people," and he did stress how religion was used by the ruling class to justify the status quo and to pacify the oppressed classes. However, Marx's theory is more complicated than is usually appreciated, in that he also recognized religion as an implicit protest against the status quo, a longing for a better world which indirectly indicts the actual world.

Now just *how* do such theories constitute an objection to religious belief? On the surface, it is hard to see. It is difficult to find, for example, arguments in Marx's writings against the reasonableness of belief in God; Marx seems just to assume that God does not exist, and, on that assumption, to construct a theory about why people believe in God. Marx's procedure is typical of sociological critics of religion, who often simply assume answers to the significant philosophical questions about religious belief.

Perhaps the difficulty that sociology is thought to pose for religious belief stems from the assumption that a sociological account gives a *complete* explanation of the origin of religious belief, and that this makes it possible to explain purported religious experiences and revelations in a purely naturalistic manner. But one must be careful here. Both Durkheim and Marx have given us provocative theories about the social functions that religion fulfills, but from this alone it would be fallacious to draw any conclusions about the *truth* of religion. To infer that religious beliefs are false on the basis of an account of their sociological origins is to commit what logicians call the *genetic fallacy*. Strictly speaking, an account of the origins or genesis of a belief implies nothing about the truth or falsity of that belief. A belief that originates in strange or unusual circumstances may still be true; if evidence is offered for a belief, that evidence should be examined and not dismissed merely because of the belief's suspicious parentage. It would seem then that the evidence religious believers adduce for their faith should be taken seriously, regardless of whether the origins of those beliefs can be explained in sociological terms. If it turns out that no rational basis for such a belief exists, then a sociological account of why people continue to believe may be in order, but such an account would again presuppose, and not establish, the unreasonableness of religious belief.[7]

Furthermore, there are strong reasons for thinking that religious beliefs cannot be explained completely in sociological terms. Against Durkheim's theory of God as a symbolization of the power and authority of society, it has been pointed out that such a theory accounts neither for the universal scope of the teachings of the higher religions nor for the power religion has to criticize society in a prophetic manner.[8] Against Marx, one can note that though religious beliefs have often been used to justify social oppression, they have also frequently provided the motivation for those who stood up against oppression—the abolitionists in nineteenth-century America being a good example.

In any case, the fact that religion fulfills certain important functions in society is not surprising and should not be particularly threatening to the believer. Actually, the believer has a great deal to gain from sociological studies of religion. It is extremely important to understand the way social context shapes religion and the way religion influences society.

Freud and the challenge of psychology. A host of psychologists have theorized about the psychological origins and functions of religious belief, but none has been so influential as Sigmund Freud (1856-1939). In his book *The Future of an Illusion,* Freud attempted to explain both the origins of religious ideas and why they have continued to be popular.

Freud's theory, which overlaps sociological theories to some degree, views religious beliefs as fulfilling several deep, psychological needs. First, religion helps allay our fears of the uncontrolled order of nature by personifying that order, or at least by viewing nature as being under personal control. Second, religion helps us accept the costs of civilization, which Freud sees as taking a toll on our natural biological urges. Religion both sanctifies the rules and institutions of society and promises future rewards which compensate for the pain these restrictions bring us. In our dealings with both nature and society, Freud sees religion as an expression of the longing for a *father figure.* As in the sociological theory, human beings create God in their own image to satisfy their own needs. For Freud, religion is an illusion—an illusion that produces some positive benefits, to be sure, but one that places human beings in an immature, infantile state.

Once more, it appears that even if Freud's account is accepted, it does not follow that religious belief is false. It is not surprising to the religious believer that religion fulfills important psychological functions. If Freud is right, then humans have a deep need to believe in God. But surely the existence of such a need does not show that God does not exist. Indeed, many religious believers would accept much of Freud's account of the importance of early childhood experiences—and of one's relationship to one's father, in particular—in developing beliefs about God. For them the human family is a divinely designed institution, whose function may be, in part, to give humans some idea of what God is like and some inclination to believe in him.

Strictly speaking, then, Freud's theories about the origin of religious belief are not objections to religious belief, and to think otherwise is, once more, to commit the genetic fallacy. It is possible, however, to object to religious belief on the basis of Freud's ideas. (A similar objection can be generated from sociological theories.) Even though one cannot infer the falsity of a belief on the basis of its origin without committing the genetic fallacy, the psychological origins or functions of a belief may provide one with negative evidence if one also has some additional information about those origins. A particular belief held for peculiar psychological reasons may still be true, but if it is known that beliefs held for that kind of reason are usually or generally false, then one has some evidence that the belief in question is false as well. A Freudian might reason, then, as follows: Religious beliefs are held solely to satisfy deep psychological needs. Beliefs which are held solely to satisfy deep psychological needs are usually false. Therefore, religious beliefs are probably false.

This argument does not seem particularly strong, however, as both premises are open to challenge. Religious beliefs do satisfy deep psychological needs, but it is hard to see how one could establish that this is their *sole* basis. Certainly, one could not do so without a careful examination of the evidence given in favor of religious belief, something notably lacking from Freud's account. Also, it should be noted that religious belief is not always comforting or psychologically reassuring. Many people find religious ideas unsettling and challenging.

The second premise also seems questionable. People have, for example, deep psychological needs to believe in the reality and constancy of the physical world and the reliability of experience as a guide to the future. It would be absurd to question these beliefs because of this psychological fact, even though philosophers in fact find it difficult to justify these beliefs.

Finally, it is perhaps worth noting that the kind of reductionism that characterizes many psychological and sociological accounts of religious belief is actually a two-edged sword. Sociologists of knowledge can give accounts of the social origins of atheistic beliefs, as well as religious beliefs. If believers sometimes show a deep psychological need to believe in God, nonbelievers sometimes show an equally deep psychological need to reject any authority over them and to assert themselves as their own lords and masters.[9]

Cognitive psychology and the explanation of religion. In recent decades, the dominant critique of religion emerging from the social sciences has focused on the cognitive faculties responsible for religious beliefs.[10] A plethora of recent books—including Daniel Dennett's *Breaking the Spell: Religion as a Natural Phenomenon* and Dawkins's *The God Delusion*,[11] to name two of the more prominent titles—aim to debunk religious belief by revealing its ostensively evolutionary origins. The basic idea is that if religious belief can be shown to be purely natural—in particular, a product of Darwinian natural selection—then it will thereby have been demonstrated that religion is a delusion, and that continued belief in it, once we understand its true origins, is irrational.

To develop the critique, we begin with the basics of a dominant model in contemporary cognitive psychology of religion. The general picture that has emerged is this. In the course of our evolutionary development, humans acquired certain fitness-enhancing cognitive faculties. One such faculty, easily activated by various environmental stimuli, produces belief in the existence of agents. The key term here is "easily:" the faculty in question produces such beliefs with only minimal environmental prodding and is thus termed the "hypersensitive agency detection device" (HADD). In the presence of certain stimuli—for example, the sound of rustling leaves—HADD produces beliefs about the existence of agents—for example, that someone is approaching—and it produces them without the involvement of any reflection or inferential reasoning (such beliefs are thus "immediate"). Once activated, another faculty, called the "Theory of Mind," goes into effect, attributing various cognitive states (beliefs, emotions, intentions, volitions, etc.) to the agent that HADD postulates.

It is not hard to guess where this is headed. These two faculties—HADD and the Theory of Mind—collectively constitute "the god-faculty," the faculty that results in belief in all kinds of supernatural entities. The ubiquity of such beliefs is accounted for by the fact that the god-faculty is universal (i.e., possessed by all humans), and the universality of the faculty is accounted for in evolutionary terms. Proponents of this account of religious belief disagree with one another about whether the god beliefs are themselves fitness-enhancing, but agree that the components of the god-faculty (HADD and the Theory of Mind) certainly gave our evolutionary ancestors a survival edge, which explains why we possess the god-faculty today.

Various kinds of responses to this account of religious belief are possible. One response is to point out the dearth of empirical evidence supporting theories in evolutionary psychology and the resulting, highly speculative nature of all such accounts of the origin of religious beliefs. Much like what we find in Marx and Freud, we seem to have here what philosophers call a "just-so" story: an account of the origins of something that, if true, would explain the thing's existence, but for which no independent evidence is given.

But even if this account of the origin of religious belief is accurate, how is it supposed to function as a *critique*? This question points to a second response: one may concede—at least for the sake of argument—the evolutionary account of the god faculty and its role in the formation of religious beliefs, but then argue that nothing of any theological significance follows from this. In particular, nothing about the truth or rationality of religious belief follows. Contra Dawkins and Dennett, there is no good reason to assume that religious belief is false or irrational just because it has a "natural" origin. After all, if Darwinism is true, then *all* our faculties have a natural origin. But surely Darwinists do not wish to claim that all beliefs that are products of some cognitive faculty are unjustified, for this leads immediately to radical skepticism.

What the critic needs, then, is some other premise to bridge the gap between "Religion has a natural origin" and "Religious beliefs are false/delusory/unjustified," one that does not imply that obviously justified beliefs—for example, beliefs about basic scientific or moral truths—are unjustified. But what could this premise be?[12] No plausible candidate seems forthcoming, and thus the argument from evolutionary psychology appears to be a failure.

This failure should not be surprising, especially in light of the conclusion we reached in chapter three: that evolution and theism need not be mutually exclusive. Particularly if evolution is viewed as divinely guided, there is no reason to think that revealing the evolutionary basis of a "god faculty"—if there be such a thing—proves that religious belief is false or irrational or even unjustified. In fact, there is some reason to conclude just the opposite. Perhaps such a faculty is exactly what God intended humans to possess, in order that a basic awareness of his existence would be available to all. We will return to a variation of this idea in chapter eight, when we discuss Reformed epistemology.

Religious Uses of Modern Atheism?

The bulk of the discussion in this chapter has been critical responses to the various kinds of critiques of religion that have been constructed in the name of science or modernity. But perhaps we should end on a slightly different note. Despite all that has been said in response to these critiques, there is, perhaps, wisdom in believers' being willing to listen to and take seriously a *certain version* of the sociological critique—a version, found at various points in the writings of Marx and Freud, which aims to debunk not the veracity of religious belief but rather the true motivations of religious believers. In a fascinating study Merold Westphal has argued that Christians, in particular, can be edified by recognizing that the criticisms of Marx and Freud—and of Nietzsche as well—that are aimed at religious believers are in fact *"all too true all too much of the time,"* despite any logical or factual infelicities their broader positions may contain.[13] What these three thinkers share in common, Westphal notes, is "their joint practice of the *hermeneutics of suspicion, the deliberate attempt to expose the self-deceptions involved in hiding our actual operative motives from ourselves, individually or collectively, in order not to notice how and how much our behavior and our beliefs are shaped by values we profess to disown.*"[14] Their critiques, in short, can be seen as directing our attention toward *instrumental religion*—religion that serves our own purposes in ways that we would like not to admit, religion that is even "idolatrous by our own standards."[15]

Marx does this by highlighting the way that religion is often used by those in power (often unconsciously) to subtly justify and preserve the status quo, which—in a way that is none too Christian—serves their own best interests at the expense of the marginalized and the underprivileged. Freud draws attention to the way that religion is used on an individual basis both to fulfill our unconscious desire that nature can be tamed and to deal with the destructive, violent and perverse desires of our own hearts (in Freud's terminology, the id) without having to admit these tendencies to ourselves. Nietzsche exposes the way that Judeo-Christian religion, in particular, with its ostensive glorification of humility, justice and love for one's neighbor, may be used as a front for a kind of power grab, with its true motivations lying in weakness, envy and a desire for revenge.[16] His critique reveals the way that true religion so quickly becomes Pharisaism, in which religion is used to separate people into categories of "us" (the good, the righteous, those favored by God) and "them" (the evil ones, the sinners, those destined for judgment), in order to elevate ourselves, both in our own eyes and in the eyes of other people.

Westphal's thesis is that within the scathing denunciations of religion found in Marx, Freud and Nietzsche there is a *biblical* critique—a critique of false religion that is repeated throughout Scripture by both the prophets and Jesus. Because of this, Christians ought to listen carefully to these critiques, examining their own beliefs and motives carefully, and taking to heart the criticisms of these "masters of suspicion," wherever their allegations are found to "stick." Believers are thereby better able to guard against instrumental religion and self-deception, the complex phenomenon whereby one hides from oneself the truth that, on one level, one knows, because the truth is too painful or personally incriminating to acknowledge. Self-deception and false religion are much more dangerous—both to individual spiritual well-being and to the collective preservation of the kind of Christianity that Jesus himself taught—than any atheistic argument for God's nonexistence. As such, there are occasions on which the believer dismisses the objections of her critics at her own peril.

None of this is to deny that Christians ought to seek to refute "evidential atheism"—that is, the kind of atheism that contends that belief in God is unwarranted or irrational because it is not supported by sufficient evidence—wherever they find it. But the "atheism of suspicion" found in Marx, Freud and Nietzsche calls not for immediate refutation, but first for self-examination. In this way, modern atheism can have an important, perhaps indispensable, religious use.

7

The Problem of Evil

Of all the objections to theism presented by atheists, the most celebrated and oft-rehearsed, by far, is the problem of evil and suffering. Debates about evolution and the like notwithstanding, most reflective theists would likely agree that objections to belief in God posed by the occurrence of evil and suffering present a far more serious challenge than do objections from science. (In fact, one of the most popular lines of objection to theistic evolution is really a version of the problem of evil; it asks, How could a perfectly loving God employ a means of creation that proceeds by way of the systematic destruction of the weakest and most vulnerable creatures?) A distinction must be drawn, however, between the problem of evil as a philosophical *objection* to religious belief and the problem as a concerned *question*.

Some philosophers have put forward arguments from evil which purport to show that God does not exist or that belief in God is unreasonable. To such philosophical attacks, philosophical responses are appropriate. However, many people—believers and nonbelievers alike—are bothered by evil. When they are faced with suffering, on their own part or on the part of others, they may pose an agonizing *Why?* A philosophical argument is often the last thing such a person wants to hear; such an argument may appear irritatingly superficial or even callous. The person wants compassion and empathy, and the proper response may simply be to listen and try to share the other's grief and questions. At such times the problem of evil calls more for pastoral care than for philosophical debate.

The philosophical problem of evil, on the other hand, can be posed briefly and sharply. It appears to many people that a perfectly good, all-knowing and all-powerful being, were he to exist, would not allow the kinds or quantity of evil and suffering that exists in our world. The underlying assumption of this argument is the intuition—common to many atheists and theists alike—that a good being eliminates evil as far as it is able to. God, being omniscient, should be aware of every instance of evil and suffering; being perfectly good, he would presumably want to eliminate all evil; being omnipotent, he should be able to do just that. If there were a God, therefore, one would expect not to find any evil in the world. Since one does find evil—and quite a bit of it—God must not exist. In this way, the existence of evil and suffering is thought to undermine the rationality of belief in God.

Types of Evil, Versions of the Problem and Types of Responses

The evils in the world which this argument takes as its basis are usually divided into two types. *Moral evil* is all the evil which is due to the actions of free, morally responsible beings. Murders, rapes and the hunger caused by social injustice would be examples of moral evil. *Natural evil* (or *nonmoral evil*) is all the evil that is not (or at least does not appear to be) due to the actions of morally responsible beings, such as the pain and suffering caused by natural disasters and many diseases. It might seem strange to call pain and suffering a kind of "evil"—many people are accustomed to using the term only to refer to moral evil—but we should not be tripped up by this terminological usage. The reason for the label becomes clear when we consider that pain and suffering of any kind seem—at face value—out of place in a world governed by an all-powerful, all-knowing, and perfectly good and loving God. The problem of evil thus extends to pain and suffering of any kind, including that resulting from "natural" causes.

A distinction must also be made between two types of arguments from evil. Some philosophers believe that the existence of evil constitutes a proof that God does not exist. On their view the occurrence of evil and the existence of God are logically incompatible: it is a contradiction to claim both that a perfectly good, all-knowing, all-powerful being exists *and* that evil exists. This is called the *logical form* of the problem of evil.

Other atheistic philosophers make a more modest claim. They are willing to admit that God's existence is logically compatible with the occurrence of evil: they concede that it is *possible* that a perfectly good, all-knowing, all-powerful being might have reasons for allowing evil. However, they allege that, given the actual types and quantity of evil that we find in the world, it is *unlikely* or *improbable* that this is so in every case. Hence, the occurrence of evil, though it does not prove that God does not exist, renders his existence unlikely or improbable. This line of argument is called the *evidential form* of the problem of evil. We will address each of these versions of the problem in turn.

Theistic responses to the problem of evil can also be divided into two types. The more ambitious type of response is a *theodicy*, which attempts to explain why God actually allows evil. A theodicy tries to *show* that God is justified in allowing evil; it lays out the reasons why God allows evil and tries to show that those reasons are good ones. A more modest type of response, called a *defense*, tries to argue that God may have reasons for allowing evil that we do not or cannot know. A defense does not try to explain why God actually allows evil but argues that it is reasonable to believe that God has good reasons, even if we are not in a position to discern what they are. A defense may give various explanations as possible reasons why God allows evil, but without claiming that those reasons are necessarily God's actual ones.

There are certain ways of resolving the problem of evil that, while perhaps *logically* adequate, are not genuine options for the orthodox theist.[1] One way is simply to deny the reality of evil, to view evil as an illusion. This view—aside from the difficulty that it must still face the problem of the evil of a widespread, illusory belief—is simply not consistent with Christianity, Judaism and Islam, which take evil as something which is all too real and which must be treated with great seriousness.

Another way of resolving the problem would be to regard God as limited in either power or knowledge or goodness or all three. Perhaps evil is due to a recalcitrant material that God is doing his best to straighten out, or perhaps some recalcitrant streak in God's own character that he is still trying to tame. The former option was urged by the school of Boston Personalism in the early twentieth century, while both have been asserted by various process theologians. Such "finite theisms" are perhaps worthy of consideration, but it is clear that any such position represents a major modification of traditional theism, and, as such, an abandonment of essential elements of the great theistic religions. Before accepting some such view, it is wise to see whether orthodox theism has within it the resources to solve the problem of evil.

The Logical Form of the Problem

One of the most well-known statements of the logical form of the problem of evil comes from J. L. Mackie, who claims that it is "positively irrational" to affirm, on the one hand, that God exists and is wholly good and omnipotent, and yet to admit, on the other, that evil exists.[2] Mackie admits that the contradiction is not immediately obvious; to show it, he says, some additional premises must be added which spell out the meaning of terms like "good," "evil" and "omnipotent."

> These additional principles are that good is opposed to evil, in such a way that a good thing always eliminates evil as far as it

> can, and that there are no limits to what an omnipotent thing can do. From these it follows that a good omnipotent thing eliminates evil completely, and then the propositions that a good omnipotent thing exists and that evil exists are incompatible.[3]

Mackie is claiming that the proposition that God exists, combined with his additional premises, logically implies that evil does not exist, which contradicts the (obviously true) proposition that evil does exist.

Theistic responses to Mackie's argument (and to other similar arguments) have typically focused on the claim that a good being always eliminates evil as far as it can. Why should we accept this additional premise? There seem to be quite a few circumstances in which a good being allows evil to occur which could be eliminated, for the reason that eliminating the evil would also eliminate a good which is great enough to "outweigh" the evil allowed. For example, a heroic soldier might fall on a live grenade to save his comrades. His death is surely an evil (in the sense that we are using this term), yet his action in bringing about this evil is nonetheless the action of a good person. Perhaps by diving into a trench, the soldier could save his own life and prevent that evil, but to do so would result in a greater evil (the death of all his comrades). So the good that is brought about by his action outweighs the evil.

It does not seem to be true, then, that a good being always eliminates evil as far as it can. What is true, perhaps, is that a good being always eliminates evil as far as it can *without the loss of a greater good or the allowance of a worse evil.* Almost all contemporary theodicies base their arguments on this type of "greater-good" principle. The evil that God permits is justified because allowing that evil makes possible the achievement of a greater good or the prevention of a worse evil.

But at this point we must be careful how we employ the "greater-good" relation in dealing with the problem of evil. The critic is likely to object that an omnipotent being must be able to eliminate evil completely, without any net loss of good or increase of evil, for, unlike our heroic soldier, an omnipotent being is supposed to be able to do anything. God, if truly omnipotent, would never find himself in a position in which some good is "out of reach" unless he allows some evil to occur. He could never find himself in a position analogous to the heroic soldier, for example, because he could always bring about the good result directly (e.g., by causing the grenade not to explode or by causing the soldiers to be miraculously unharmed in the blast). The "greater-good" principle thus applies only to beings of limited power, like ourselves.

The response to this has traditionally been that not even an omnipotent being can do literally anything. One limitation on omnipotence which has generally been accepted by theists, as we noted in chapter two, is that even God cannot do what is broadly logically impossible. An omnipotent being cannot create a square circle or bring it about that 2 + 2 = 5, because these contradictory states of affairs are not genuine possibilities.

Whether this point is of any relevance to the present discussion, however, depends on whether the allowance of certain evils is *logically necessary* for certain goods to be achieved. But it seems plausible that this is so. Let us define a *second-order good* as a good that logically requires the existence (or at least the possibility) of some evil in order to be realized. Various kinds of goods and evils have been claimed to be related in this way, giving rise to various types of theodicies. For example, certain kinds of moral virtues seem to logically require certain evils. Courage seems inconceivable without the possibility of harm. Sympathy would be impossible apart from the suffering of others. Perhaps much of the evil in the world—particularly much of the natural evil—is necessary for human beings to have the opportunity to cultivate the moral virtues, which are second-order goods. Perhaps, furthermore, these second-order goods are of such great value that their realization justifies the allowance of the evils whose existence (or possibility) they require. The idea certainly does not seem far-fetched, and it can be developed into a theodicy: the world has been designed by God to be, first and foremost, an environment that enables and facilitates each individual's moral and spiritual development. This solution is termed a *soul-making theodicy.*[4]

The difficulties with soul-making theodicies are plentiful. One problem is that not all natural evils seem to contribute to any greater good—the suffering of some animals, for example. Consider a scenario in which, far away from any human witness, a lightning strike starts a forest fire that burns a fawn severely and causes it to experience a slow, agonizing death.[5] Surely events like this occur, but why would a loving God allow them? There appears to be no second-order good for which this evil is necessary. A second problem is that—in addition to making possible various second-order goods, such as courage and sympathy—evils such as pain and suffering also make possible second-order *evils*, such as cowardice and maliciousness. Allowing such evils as pain and suffering does not, then, always lead to a greater good, and it even opens the door for certain evils that otherwise would be impossible. Or, to put the point differently, if second-order goods suffice to justify "first-order" evils like pain and suffering, the problem of evil simply switches its focus to the existence of second-order evils, such as cowardice and maliciousness. By itself, the soul-making theodicy seems unable to identify any greater good that could justify God's allowance of these second-order evils.[6]

Because of this last problem, most theists who advocate a soul-making theodicy incorporate into their view another kind of theodicy as well: the *free will theodicy.* According to this solution, the reason that second-order evils occur, such as acts of cowardice and maliciousness, is that human beings make bad use of their freedom. The resulting evil is due to human wickedness, not to God.

But why should God give humans free will, and why should he allow them to use it so badly? The traditional answer is that moral freedom is a great good which outweighs the possibility of evil that its existence requires. More specifically, God allows humans to act freely because, without doing so, humans could not be morally responsible agents, capable of freely doing good by responding to and loving their neighbors and their Creator. In creating human beings, God desired to make creatures who would freely love and serve him. The "love" of a robot who can do nothing else is not worth much. The highest expression of love is communion with God, the greatest possible good for a human being. But for God to leave us genuinely free to act is for him to allow us the possibility of misusing that freedom—allowing us, for example, to choose to perform acts of great cowardice or maliciousness. True freedom thus involves great risk, but also the possibility of a great good which can be achieved in no other way. In this manner the soul-making theodicy and free will theodicy work together to account for both first-order and second-order evil.

But why—the critic might ask—couldn't God give humans free will and guarantee that they always use their freedom wisely? Upon first encounter the critic's question strikes many as nonsensical: surely, it is thought, if humans are genuinely free, then sometimes they will put that freedom to bad use. If God had created a world in which it was guaranteed that no one would ever do anything wrong, then the "freedom" of his creatures would not have been real; it would have been some kind of pseudofreedom.

But before we dismiss the critic too quickly, we should consider the way that Mackie formulates the objection:

> I should ask this: if God has made men such that in their free choices they sometimes prefer what is good and sometimes what is evil, why could he not have made men such that they always freely choose the good? If there is no logical impossibility in a man's freely choosing the good on one, or on several, occasions, there cannot be a logical impossibility in his freely choosing the good on every occasion. God was not, then, faced with a choice between making innocent automata and

> making beings who, in acting freely, would sometimes go wrong: there was open to him the obviously better possibility of making beings who would act freely but always go right. Clearly, his failure to avail himself of this possibility is inconsistent with his being both omnipotent and wholly good.[7]

What Mackie's objection highlights is this: a scenario in which God creates free creatures who always freely choose to do what is right does seem to be a logically possible state of affairs and thus a component of a logically possible "world," a maximal possible way things could have been. But if God is omnipotent, then it has usually been thought that he can bring about anything that is logically possible: omnipotence implies that God can actualize any possible world. It seems to follow that it was within God's power to create a world containing free creatures but no evil. Thus the presence of evil in the world, if this line of thinking is correct, entails that an omnipotent, perfectly good God does not exist.

However, Alvin Plantinga has developed a powerful argument that Mackie's objection is not sound. The heart of Plantinga's argument rests on the libertarian view of freedom, which implies that if a person has a genuinely free choice, what the person will do in that situation is solely up to the person and not up to God. Suppose some individual is faced with a choice as to whether he will perform some immoral act, such as accepting a bribe. On Plantinga's (fictional) example, a politician named Curley has accepted a bribe of $35,000.[8] That is, in the imagined world it is true that Curley has actually accepted the bribe. Suppose, however, Curley had been offered a lesser sum, say only $20,000. Would he have accepted this lesser bribe? Many philosophers would agree that one of the following propositions (but not both) is true:

(1) If Curley had been offered $20,000, he would have accepted the bribe.

(2) If Curley had been offered $20,000, he would have rejected the bribe.

Notice that both propositions (1) and (2) seem logically possible, and thus there is a possible world in which Curley accepts the lesser bribe and also a possible world in which he rejects the lesser bribe. Suppose that (1) is true: Curley would freely accept the lesser bribe if it were offered. In that case, there is a logically possible world that God cannot actualize: namely, the one in which (2) is true and Curley rejects the bribe. If, on the other hand, (2) is true and Curley would freely reject the bribe, then the possible world in which proposition (1) is true turns out to be the world that God cannot actualize. Either way, it turns out that if we assume libertarian free will, and we assume that either proposition (1) or (2) must be true, then there are logically possible worlds which even an omnipotent being cannot bring into existence.[9]

This conclusion directly undermines Mackie's objection, which rests on the assumption that there is a logically possible world in which free beings exist but never do evil. Plantinga's response is to concede that there is such a logically possible world, but to claim that we have no reason to think that this world is one that is within God's power to create. There are some logically possible worlds God cannot create; whether God can create a particular world depends on the choices made by the free creatures in it.

Perhaps Mackie might respond at this point by claiming that God, making use of his "middle knowledge" about what free creatures will do in various situations, should only have actualized free creatures who would never do evil. However, even if God does possess middle knowledge (and we saw earlier that there may be problems with such a view), how do we know that there are possible free creatures who, if God created them, would never misuse their freedom? It seems at least possible that all the free beings God could actualize would misuse their freedom at some time. (Plantinga calls this condition "transworld depravity," since a creature with this condition will do some evil in any possible world in which that creature exists.)[10]

The upshot is this. It seems clearly possible that God could have faced this scenario in which all the creatures he could create have transworld depravity, and if he had faced it, then any world he actualized containing free creatures would also (eventually) have contained evil. On the assumption that a world with both free creatures and evil is better than a world with neither, God was justified in creating free creatures, even though he knew full well that in doing so the result would be (eventually) a "fallen" world.

What this scenario shows is that God and evil are logically compatible. Note that Plantinga is not claiming that God *in fact* faced this scenario. He is claiming only that it is *possible* that God faced it. This is all Plantinga needs, because Mackie has asserted that God and evil are logically incompatible—in other words, that there is no possible way that the world could have been such that God and evil both exist. Plantinga's argument is a free will *defense:* it does not state what God's actual reasons are for allowing evil but only what they could be. God's actual reasons for allowing evil may be ones that we do not know and perhaps could not know.

It should be noted that difficulties for a free will *theodicy* (which is more ambitious than a free will defense) remain. Obviously, such a theodicy is no more valid than the underlying theory of free will it embodies, and, as we have encountered on more than one occasion, the debate between compatibilists and incompatibilists is ongoing, and it is one that we cannot hope to resolve here.[11] Another difficulty is that, as we have developed it so far, a free will theodicy by itself appears to account only for moral evil. To account for natural evil, the free will argument must be extended in one of three ways. One way is to combine it with another theodicy, such as a soul-making theodicy, which accounts for natural evil. Recall, however, that this combination still faced difficulties in accounting for certain kinds of natural evil: namely, those that seem to bear no relation to human free will (such as animal suffering). A second way would be to see natural evil as the work of superhuman free beings, such as Satan and his angels; this thinking converts natural evil into moral evil. A third possibility would be to see natural evil as in some way a consequence of moral evil, perhaps by interpreting it as a divine judgment on a fallen race. There is biblical support for the idea that the current state of nature is "unnatural," in the sense that it is a consequence of sin, not an expression of God's original plan or intention for it (see Gen 3:17-19; Rom 8:19-23).

Regardless of which option one selects, critics of theism will question one's basis for claiming to *know* that natural evil should be viewed in that way. It must be admitted that, as full-fledged theodicies, neither free will arguments alone nor such arguments taken in conjunction with a soul-making argument can be established conclusively. When all is said and done, it is difficult for the theist to be confident that she truly understands why God allows all the evil we find in the world.

Fortunately for the theist, though, it is not necessary to have a full-fledged theodicy to rebut the logical form of the problem of evil. For the charge of the atheist, in this case, is that theism is self-contradictory. To rebut this charge, it is not necessary to *know* God's actual reasons for allowing evil or to be able to explain why God allows the evils he does. It is sufficient to know that there are *possible* reasons why an all-good, omnipotent being might allow evil, if one wishes to show that the occurrence of evil and the existence of God are not *logically* contradictory. (It is for this reason that Plantinga's response to Mackie is a free will defense and not a free will theodicy.)

As theodicies, the soul-making and free will arguments may have their limitations, but their value in producing a defense against the logical form of the problem of evil is formidable. The free will argument, for example, shows that it is not necessarily true that a good being always eliminates all the evil it can, or that an omnipotent being could eliminate all evil without the loss of any greater good. And yet the atheist needs some such proposition to prove that the existence of God and evil are logically contradictory: specifically, she needs some proposition that is necessarily true and that, combined with the fact that evil exists, entails that God does not exist. No one, so far, has been able to do this. The charge of contradiction that Mackie and others bring is a strong one, and the burden of proof is on them to show exactly what the contradiction is. Unless they can do so, there is no good reason to conclude that the existence of evil *proves* that there is no God.

The Evidential Form of the Problem

In light of the failure of atheists to produce such a proposition, the majority consensus among philosophers today is that the logical form of the problem of evil is a failure. For this reason the main focus of the discussion has turned in recent decades to the evidential form of the problem. In some ways this marks a retreat on the atheist's part to a weaker position, but it is one that is nonetheless potentially damaging to the theist. Proponents of the evidential argument admit that theism is logically consistent and that the existence of evil does not in itself disprove the existence of God. The charge they make is that the existence of evil—and, more specifically, the kinds and quantity of evil that we actually find in the world—constitutes powerful evidence against God's existence.  Put differently, the evil that we find renders it *unlikely* that God exists, and thus it provides us with good reason for not believing in God.

The evidential form of the problem of evil is best understood as a response to the "greater-good" theodicies sketched in the last section. The atheist here admits that it is possible for a perfectly good, omniscient, omnipotent being to allow evil, if by doing so a greater good is achieved that could not be achieved in any other way. So the mere existence of evil does not contradict God's existence. However, the atheist will contend that much of the actual evil that we observe in the world is *pointless:* it does not lead to any greater good, or it is not, at any rate, logically necessary for the achievement of any greater good. A good God—by the very definition of "good"—would not allow pointless evil. The argument can be summarized as follows:

(1) If God exists, he does not allow any pointless evil.
(2) Probably, there is some pointless evil in the world.
(3) Therefore, God probably does not exist.[12]

The qualifying term "probably" is important. The atheist does not presume to be able to *prove* that there are genuinely pointless evils in the world; she can admit that it is always *possible* that God has some justifying reason for allowing the evil that is beyond our ability to comprehend. But she thinks that this is improbable for the simple reason that it clearly *appears* to us that there *are* pointless evils. The critic will note that here, just like everywhere else in life, we must make our best judgments based on the way things appear to be. Given that there appear to be pointless evils, the most rational conclusion to draw is that a perfectly good and omnipotent God probably does not exist.

In responding to the evidential form of the problem, the theist can try to rely, once again, on the theodicies we examined in the last section, as well as others that have been proposed.[13] But suppose one does not find any of these arguments convincing. It must not be forgotten that evil is a problem felt by the believer as well as the nonbeliever. Many believers find the occurrence of many evils in the world—especially those that seem particularly egregious or horrendous—baffling and troubling. They wonder why God allows these things, for they admit that these evils do appear to be pointless. What then can the believer say?

Two things, at least. First, the believer can try to refute the second premise by challenging the reasons used to support it. Recall that the reason given by atheists for thinking that it is likely or probable that there are pointless evils is simply this: it *appears* that there are pointless evils. The claim that it appears that there are some pointless evils, however, is open to challenge. Stephen Wykstra has argued that this claim violates a basic epistemic principle, called the *Condition of Reasonable Epistemic Access* (CORNEA, for short).[14] What CORNEA states, in a nutshell, is that one is justified in making a claim like "It appears that there are no Xs" only if one is justified in believing that, if there *were* any Xs, one would be in a position to perceive them.

This is best seen by way of an example.[15] Suppose that someone opened the garage door, turned on the light, took a quick glance around and, on the basis of what he saw, declared, "It appears that there are no dogs in the garage." He would be justified in making this claim, because—assuming there is nothing strange going on in this scenario—if there were any dogs in the garage, a quick glance would be sufficient for him to see them. But suppose this same person opened the garage door, turned on the light, took a quick glance around and, on the basis of what he saw, declared, "It appears that there are no fleas in the garage." In this case his claim would *not* be justified. Taking a quick glance around the garage does not suffice to justify one in making this kind of claim, because it is common knowledge that if there *were* any fleas in the garage, one likely would not be able to perceive them with just a quick glance.

The general lesson here is that one is not justified in claiming that it appears that there are no Xs if one has reason to believe that, in one's present epistemic state, one is not in a position to be able to perceive any Xs that might be there. When this is applied to the discussion of the evidential argument, the point is this. Given that God is both omniscient and transcendent, there is every reason to believe that God is privy to a vast amount of knowledge about the relations between good and evil of which we are ignorant. We have reason to believe, then, that for any allegedly pointless evil, if there *were* some justifying reason that God had for allowing it, we very likely would not be in a position to perceive it. If God exists, it is virtually certain that many of his reasons are inscrutable to us. Consequently, we are in no position to claim, for any actual evil that we observe, that that evil even *appears* to serve no greater good.[16] The claim "It appears that there are some pointless evils" is unjustified because it violates CORNEA. But without this claim, premise (2) is unfounded. This response to the evidential argument is sometimes called the *cognitive limitation defense*.

There is a second response to the evidential argument available to the believer—one that ties into the first response nicely, without being as technical. The theist can state that she believes God has reasons for allowing evil, even if she does not know what those reasons are. The believer's evidence for thinking that God has justifying reasons for allowing evil will simply be her evidence for God's existence and goodness. If one has good reasons for believing in a benevolent and loving God, then one is justified in believing that God has good reasons for allowing evil.

To appreciate the force of this kind of response, consider the following argument, which inverts the previous, atheistic argument:

(1) If God exists, he does not allow any pointless evil.
(2) Probably, God exists.
(3) Therefore, probably, there is no pointless evil in the world.

This strategy of turning an argument on its head—sometimes called a *G. E. Moore shift*, after the early twentieth-century philosopher who made it famous—results, every time, in an argument that is just as valid as the original. Which argument is to be preferred in this particular case? The answer requires that an individual make a judgment about her total evidential situation. Does one have more evidence that God exists, or does one have more evidence that pointless evils exist?

Most would admit that the existence of evil is a problem for the theist; it does "count against" the existence of God, in the sense that it provides prima facie evidence that God does not exist. (Note, however, that Wykstra's argument could be used to challenge even this assumption.) Even if this is true, however, the important question is whether this negative evidence is sufficient to count *decisively* against God's existence (whether it provides what we might call *ultima facie* evidence). If one has strong reasons for believing in God and for believing him to be good, then evil will be regarded as a difficulty, since one does not understand why God allows evil, but not as a decisive difficulty. After all, as we have just discussed, it seems highly doubtful that finite human beings, with our imperfect and selective understanding of the world around us, could justifiably claim to *know* that any evil really is genuinely pointless. If one had come to know God as a loving, good being—through religious experience and revelation, perhaps—one would then have powerful evidence that God must have good reasons for allowing evil, even if one had no idea what those reasons might be.

It is, in fact, in just this sort of situation that faith is called for. If the faith is to be reasonable, of course, there must be some basis for belief in God. But adherents of a religion normally claim to have evidence of this type. For example, Christians often cite the incarnation of Jesus as providing them with knowledge of God and God's character. Jesus' death and resurrection, while not an explanation of why God allows evil, are a demonstration that he loves his creatures to the point of suffering with them and for them, and that he will eventually triumph over evil by turning it to good. (More on this, shortly.) Evil, then, is a serious problem for the theist, but it is not necessarily an insurmountable one. If the theist has good reasons for believing in God, then he also has good reasons for believing that God is justified in permitting evil. In that case, the occurrence of evil is seen as a test of one's faith in God.

To the atheist, evil constitutes strong evidence against God's existence. From a theistic perspective, however, the person who doubts God because of the occurrence of evil needs one of two things. If he does not know God and God's goodness, he needs to come to know God—through experience or perhaps through special revelation—or he needs to come to know God in a fuller way. If he already knows God and God's goodness, then he needs pastoral encouragement that will help him persevere in his faith.

Horrendous Evils and the Problem of Hell

Recently, discussion of the problem of evil has turned to more specific versions of the problem, and, in some cases, to more specific kinds of solutions. Marilyn McCord Adams has challenged the assumption that the project of theodicy must provide "global and generic answers" to the problem of evil, arguing instead that, in certain cases at least, the resources of a specific religious tradition must be marshaled to address the problem adequately.[17] Adams argues that such resources are to be found in Christianity and in the doctrines of the incarnation and Christ's passion, specifically.

The need for nongeneric resources is especially apparent, Adams thinks, in the case of ***horrendous evils***, which she defines as "evils the participation in which (that is, the doing or suffering of which) constitutes prima facie reason to doubt whether the participant's life could (given their inclusion in it) be a great good to him/her on the whole."[18] Evils qualify as horrendous when they are "so destructive of meaning within an individual's life" that they seem to render the individual's life, on the whole, not worth living. Adams lists a number of examples of such evils: "the rape of a woman and axing off of her arms, psycho-physical torture whose ultimate goal is the disintegration of personality, betrayal of one's deepest loyalties, child abuse of the sort described by Ivan Karamazov, child pornography, parental incest, slow death by starvation, the explosion of nuclear bombs over populated areas."[19]

Horrendous evils stretch traditional theodicies to their breaking point, Adams thinks, because such theodicies rely so heavily on the "greater-good" principle that we discussed. How could any evil that is so destructive of a person's life possibly serve any good that is great enough to justify God's allowance of it? Adams insists that any answer that appeals to "global goods"—for example, God's actualizing the best of all possible worlds—will not do; only a solution in which the horrendous evil is "engulfed" and "defeated" *in the life of the individual who suffers it* will suffice. Evils are engulfed when their quantity in the life of a particular person is vastly outweighed by the quantity of good in that same person's life; evils are defeated in the life of a person when their existence is logically related to some greater good that the person experiences, such that the good could not have come about apart from the evil.

Adams does not try to explain precisely what kinds of individual experiences would bring this about—it is a part of her view that God's resources for defeating evil are beyond our comprehension or ability to even imagine—but thinks that it could only occur "by integrating participation in horrendous evils into a person's relationship with God."[20] She suggests, further, that within Christian soteriology, we find "possible dimensions of integration." Most importantly, perhaps, is God's act of identifying with human horrors in the act of Christ's voluntary submission to death on the cross: an event that invests all human suffering—no matter how horrendous—with significance and meaning.

It is clear that because many victims of horrendous evils die before such "engulfing" and "defeat" of evil are achieved in their lives, Adams's theodicy requires the existence of an afterlife in which such things will come to completion. She contends that God must employ incredible divine ingenuity and resourcefulness to mend these broken souls in their postmortem existence—to mend them to the extent that these victims of horrendous evil, in looking back on their "antemortem careers," will not regret or wish away even their own involvement with horrendous evil. More controversially, though, Adams's solution also requires a doctrine of *universalism:* the view that no one is eternally consigned to hell. It cannot be that anyone experiences eternal torment in hell, Adams thinks, for this would be a paradigmatic example of an undefeated horrendous evil.

The requirement of universalism is, for many Christians, an unacceptable cost of Adams's solution. The doctrine that some (perhaps many) experience in the afterlife the "second death" of eternal separation from God—whether this involves annihilation or a state of conscious suffering without end—is a deeply engrained part of traditional Christian teachings; it is considered one of the central themes of the New Testament and an integral part of the gospel message. As such, abandoning the doctrine would have serious repercussions for other key doctrines, including the doctrines of incarnation, salvation and atonement. From what is one saved if not from hell? If there is no hell, why should the matter of accepting Christ be so important or so pressing? Most orthodox Christians have judged it more reasonable to retain the doctrine of hell and wrestle with its implications rather than to abandon it and try to answer questions such as these.[21]

Yet the traditional doctrine of hell presents enormous theological and philosophical difficulties. Hell is—nearly by definition—the worst thing that any person could experience. If there is *any* evil that could befall a person such that it would make one doubt whether that person's life is, on the whole, a great good for him, it is surely the evil of being eternally consigned to hell. Thus, if hell is a genuine possibility, it constitutes the most severe version of the problem of horrendous evil. And if Adams is right that horrendous evils in general are the most difficult evils to reconcile with God's goodness, then, for those who endorse it, the doctrine of hell constitutes the single most difficult version of the problem of evil. Furthermore, endorsing the doctrine of hell prevents one from dealing with the problem of earthly horrendous evils in the way that Adams does. If universalism is denied and the traditional doctrine of hell is upheld, then one needs an alternate theodicy to explain why God allows some people to suffer to the point that (it seems) it would have been better had they never been born. Thus, hell is both the paradigmatic horrendous evil and that which undercuts an otherwise promising solution to the problem of earthly horrendous evils. The two problems are, it seems, reciprocally exacerbating.

How can the orthodox theist meet this challenge? Two solutions that have been prominent in recent discussions are (1) the doctrine of *annihilationism,* and (2) the doctrine of *mild hell.* The former is, as the name suggests, the view that God in his mercy simply annihilates those who make a final decision to reject him.[22] Variations of the annihilationist view are possible: for example, one might hold that God annihilates the lost immediately (or soon after) their earthly deaths, or one could hold instead that the lost are annihilated only after they have suffered for some finite period of time in hell (perhaps as punishment for their sins). Also, God need not be conceived as exerting some power to bring about the annihilation of any person: given the traditional doctrine of divine conservation, all God must do to bring about the annihilation of a thing is simply to cease sustaining it, for nothing possesses the power to sustain itself in existence. The annihilation of the lost is viewed as an act of mercy on God's part because, presumably, the only alternative for one who is finally and irrevocably separated from God would be an eternity of conscious suffering.

Apart from the question of whether annihilationism is biblical—an issue that will be put aside for present purposes—critics object that the view implies that certain evils remain finally undefeated in the world: at the very least, the evil of a person's being annihilated, but perhaps also any horrendous evils that person may have experienced prior to being annihilated. But proponents of the view may respond that for all we know, such earthly horrendous evils may be defeated in other ways, and the evil of a person's being annihilated could be defeated by the fact that it is necessary to avoid a worse evil (an eternity of conscious suffering).

A second solution, the doctrine of mild hell, is essentially a version of the free will theodicy.[23] It holds that hell is something freely chosen by its inhabitants (its human inhabitants, at least), rather than something to which God consigns the damned against their wills. The greater good that is served by hell is the preservation of human freedom: God respects each individual's choice to finally reject him, if the individual so chooses.

Once again, the view comes in a variety of different forms, but a prominent feature of most is that the damned actually *prefer* existence in hell to both annihilation and, surprisingly, even existence in heaven. The damned prefer hell to heaven because, in their pride, they have rejected all external authority, including that of their Creator, or they have acquired a wicked and vicious moral character that experiences the presence of a holy God as torturous (or both). C. S. Lewis expresses the view well when he writes, in *The Great Divorce*, "There are only two kinds of people in the end: those who say to God, 'Thy will be done,' and those to whom God says, in the end, '*Thy* will be done.' All that are in Hell, choose it."[24] Lewis elaborates elsewhere, in *The Problem of Pain:*

> I willingly believe that the damned are, in one sense, successful, rebels to the end; that the doors of hell are locked on the *inside*. I do not mean that the ghosts may not *wish* to come out of hell, in the vague fashion wherein an envious man "wishes" to be happy: but they certainly do not will even the first preliminary states of that self-abandonment through which alone the soul can reach any good. They enjoy forever the horrible freedom they have demanded, and are therefore self-enslaved: just as the blessed, forever submitting to obedience, become through all eternity more and more free.[25]

On this view, not only are the damned sent to hell of their own free choice, they remain in hell of their own free choice. Presumably, though, individuals could make a fully informed decision to reject heaven and embrace hell in this manner only if hell does not consist of a literal lake of fire or medieval-style torture chambers, ideas which have found their way into popular versions of the traditional doctrine of hell. (Mild hell thus stands opposed to the traditional view, sometimes termed "grim hell.") Hell is a "place" where those who have rejected God are allowed to continue to exist (presumably, a good thing in itself), and where they are given what they want: namely, to be apart from God.

One might ask whether mild hell is really hell in the traditional sense, since it does not involve literal physical torture, incessant burning and so on. The answer depends on whether one takes an objective or subjective view of the state of the people in hell. Perhaps, from the subjective view of those in hell, who after all prefer to be there, hell may not seem so terrible. But from the point of view of those who enjoy true bliss in heaven by knowing God and being part of the community of those who love God and the good, the fate of those in hell is truly dreadful, one that is aptly symbolized by the biblical pictures of hell as a place of torment. And it must be those in heaven who have a true view of such matters. In fact, part of the misery of hell may be the sad fact that those who are in hell do not even realize how miserable their condition is because they have lost the capacity to appreciate genuine happiness.

A main criticism of the mild-hell solution is that it places too high a premium on human freedom, especially in light of human frailty and cognitive limitations.[26] The solution implicitly assumes that God's relation to us is analogous to that of parents to their adolescent or adult children; that is, it assumes that we are capable, if we so choose, of making rational decisions informed by a full (or at least adequate) understanding of the consequences of our actions. But in other contexts traditional theism assumes that our relation to God is more analogous to that of very young children to their parents: our knowledge of the world is, in comparison with God's, minuscule, and our understanding of the world is likely impaired by myriad confusions and conceptual distortions. But if this is so, how can we be entrusted to make a decision that carries such enormous and irrevocable consequences? Critics allege that God's doing such a thing would be morally equivalent to a parent who places a bowl of poisoned candy in the middle of a room with a three year old, with a stern warning to the child not to eat the candy, who then leaves the room to allow the child to choose for himself whether or not to obey. Marilyn Adams argues that, in this kind of scenario, if the child disobeys, thereby bringing about his own death, then "surely the child is at most marginally to blame, even though it knew enough to obey the parent, while the parent is both primarily responsible and highly culpable."[27] Adams concludes that the value of human freedom, however great, is not enough to justify God's allowing creatures to make decisions that bring about their own final, irrevocable ruin. This is especially true, Adams thinks, in light of the fact that human agency is a developmental trait, shaped over time by many forces, and the agency of many individuals is stunted, impaired or even rendered dysfunctional by factors that are beyond those individuals' control (e.g., by traumatic experiences such as childhood sexual abuse).

In response, advocates of the mild-hell solution must insist that freedom really is so important that it justifies God's allowing even the most extreme of its misuses, namely, an agent's final rejection of God and consequent willing of her own damnation. Further, they must claim that many people—specifically, all those whom God holds accountable for their choice to finally accept or reject him—possess all that is required for them to be responsible for such a choice: they know what they are doing, they are not coerced, they understand well enough the consequences of their actions, and so on. Perhaps, if they do not possess what is required for a responsible choice in this life, some kind of illumination beyond death may be given that makes possible a genuinely free choice. In response to Adams's point that the agency of many individuals is stunted or impaired by factors beyond their control, proponents of mild hell may argue that God takes such factors into account in assessing the responsibility—and final judgment—of each individual.

This, in fact, points to a more general response that all proponents of the doctrine of hell may adopt. There is much that we do not know about hell in any detail—including its specific character as well as who will and will not be in it—so we should be cautious in the specificity of the conclusions we draw. But since we know that God is a God of love and mercy as well as justice, we can be confident that he will do what is loving and merciful as well as just. Our confidence in the character of God, then, should outweigh the confidence we have in our theories about hell, especially when it comes to the details, which God in his wisdom has chosen not to reveal to us in the Bible.

Divine Hiddenness

One further facet of the problem of evil, which has received a good deal of recent attention, focuses on the apparent fact that God's existence is not clearly manifest. The problem of divine hiddenness can be construed either as an argument for God's nonexistence or as a problem of "existential concern" for theists.[28] In the latter form, its focus is not so much God's existence but rather his nature or the nature of our relationship to him: it is a problem for theists in trying to reconcile their beliefs about divine power, knowledge and (especially) love with the fact that, at many times and for many people, God is "silent" or "hidden." To say that he is silent or hidden is to say that his existence, his presence or his self-disclosure—especially concerning his reasons for some evil that he has allowed to occur—is indiscernible or inscrutable.

The problem of divine hiddenness is a practical problem, for it is often the impetus—or at least a contributing factor—to an individual's crisis of faith. Has God not promised that all who seek will find? Why then does he not reveal himself plainly, at least to everyone who earnestly and diligently seeks to know him? Surprisingly, the hiddenness of God is something of a leitmotif in Scripture, especially in the Old Testament, explored most famously in the book of Job, but also scattered throughout the psalms and the writings of the prophets.[29] It is, like the problem of hell, a problem very much internal to orthodox theism.

The problem is closely tied to the problem of evil, for divine hiddenness is most productive of suffering for those *already* in the midst of suffering: the inability of such persons to perceive God or his purposes intensifies their suffering by making it feel to them as if God does not care, or that their sufferings are meaningless, or that God has forsaken them or does not love them, and so on. This is especially true in cases of horrendous evils, of the kind we have discussed. (The problem of divine hiddenness is, not surprisingly, a prominent theme in post-Holocaust Jewish theological literature.)

Divine hiddenness also intensifies the problem of evil by seeming to undermine a common strategy in theodicy, namely, treating the way God acts in relation to his creatures as analogous to the way loving parents act toward their children. It is often claimed that just as loving parents sometimes must subject their child to some painful experience that is for the child's own good, but that the child is unable to understand, so God sometimes allows us to experience suffering for similar reasons. Divine hiddenness complicates this type of response, because we expect loving parents to make special efforts to comfort, reassure and otherwise make their presence and love clearly known to their child during the child's ordeal, especially when the parents know that the ordeal involves suffering whose ultimate, beneficial purpose the child cannot understand. The question naturally arises, Why doesn't God always do the same for his creatures in their times of intense suffering? Of course, many individuals report feeling the presence and love of God most clearly in the midst of their trials, but it must be admitted that many others do not share this experience. Again, why doesn't God *always* make himself clearly known in such circumstances?

As a problem internal to theism, divine hiddenness is indeed perplexing. But some contend that the problem of divine hiddenness is best construed not as a puzzling feature of theism but as an argument for atheism (which is not surprising, given the ties between divine hiddenness and the problem of evil). A simple version of such an argument runs as follows: a perfectly loving God, were he to exist, would reveal himself to everyone who earnestly seeks him; but not everyone who earnestly seeks God finds him; therefore, a perfectly loving God does not exist.[30]

Both premises of the argument are open to challenge, however. Some theists contend that God has good reasons for not revealing himself to everyone who seeks him, and different theories have been developed as to what God's reasons might be. Perhaps, for example, divine hiddenness is a necessary condition for God's evoking from us a free and loving—rather than coerced—response of obedience and trust. Other theists insist that God *does* in fact reveal himself to everyone who earnestly seeks him; they then offer some account of why things appear otherwise. One common approach along these lines is to argue that ignorance of God is always culpable, so those who fail to perceive God must not, contrary to appearances, seek him *in earnest.*

It is time to take stock. We have seen that the problem of evil comes in a variety of forms, with the most difficult forms seeming to arise from within the teachings of orthodox theism itself. Nevertheless, it is not clear that any of these versions of the problem of evil is insurmountable. Both the logical and evidential forms of the problem of evil can be rebutted, and the problems generated by divine hiddenness and the traditional doctrine of hell call not for an abandonment of theism but rather, at most, a reassessment of certain theological assumptions. The problem of evil is certainly serious, especially in terms of its practical ramifications—the crises of faith often faced by those in the midst of severe trials and suffering demand wise spiritual guidance and counsel—but whatever rational evidence the problem of evil provides against theism, it falls short of being compelling.

8

Faith(s) and Reason

Our contemporary religious situation differs markedly from that faced by people a few hundred years ago. In Europe prior to the Reformation, the idea that one was faced with a plurality of religious beliefs, from which one had to choose, was foreign to the great majority of people. Religious beliefs were passed down from generation to generation. Certainly, individuals may have had questions and doubts, and people were faced with choices as to how to interpret and apply what was passed down to them, but those doubts and choices still presupposed a certain framework that could be taken for granted.

In today's world many people do not enjoy such a situation. Daily contacts through education and, perhaps most powerfully, through mass media bring home to us the existence of radically different religious options. For example, Christians face not only the in-house disagreements with other Christians that have proliferated since the Reformation but also many other world religions, as well as the secular mentality which opts for no overt religious belief at all. As a result, many people are not content to hold their beliefs simply because they were passed on to them by their parents or local church. Many are troubled by the idea that their faith is a mere provincial bias or historical accident; they want to know whether they have grounds for thinking their beliefs to be genuinely true.

Because of this, philosophy of religion, construed as critical dialogue, has taken on an increased relevance and urgency in today's world. But engaging in this dialogue is not without risk, since the outcome of such a dialogue may be merely increased doubt and confusion. This book itself could serve as an illustration of the continuing debate among philosophers about the reasonableness of belief in God, the problem of evil, the possibility of miracles, the proper analysis of religious experience and many other such topics. A crucial cluster of questions emerges as we deal with religious commitment in a pluralistic world. In a world such as ours, *can* a person commit herself decisively to a particular set of religious beliefs? *Should* a person do so? Are such commitments reasonable?

The first question is largely a psychological and sociological one, and the answer seems to be yes, at least for many people. Though a larger number of agnostics may exist now than in previous eras, great numbers of people still adhere firmly to religious worldviews. And there continue to be instances of conversion, where people who once had no faith come to believe or where people of one faith come to acquire a new faith. One must include in the group of "committed people" those who are committed atheists, as well as those who are committed religious believers. The term "secular" applies to many types of individuals, from the person who scarcely gives religion a thought, to the "evangelistic atheist" who is committed to getting people to abandon their "superstitions" and embrace an atheistic creed.

The question of most interest to the philosopher, however, is not whether it is psychologically possible to be religiously committed, positively or negatively, but whether such commitments are reasonable or morally responsible. Regarding the latter, much recent atheist literature—especially that aimed at a popular audience—contends that religion is the root cause of many, perhaps most, of the world's most pressing problems: everything from ignorance, sexism, poverty and the perpetuation of disease (and hindrance to cures) to violence, genocide and terrorism. In this vein the outspoken atheist Sam Harris alleges that "religion allows people to imagine that their concerns are moral when they are highly immoral—that is, when pressing these concerns inflicts unnecessary and appalling suffering on innocent human beings."[1] Harris lists the terrorist attacks of 9/11, Mother Teresa's opposition to contraception and abortion, and evangelical resistance to embryonic stem-cell research as paradigmatic examples. His view, in short, is that religious belief is fundamentally immoral and thus should be rejected. This type of argument is sometimes called a *pragmatic objection* to religious belief.

Harris's arguments, however—like many popular atheist arguments—tend to fall prey to the following two errors. The first error lies in committing a common fallacy, which infers "X is morally reprehensible" from "Horrible things have been done in the name of X," where X refers to some ideology or worldview. The inference is obviously fallacious, for if it were valid, it would surely indict every major ideology and worldview—including atheism—that the world has ever known. The terrorist attacks of 9/11 prove no more about the moral status of theism than the mass-murder perpetuated by Stalin proves about atheism.

A second common error of such arguments lies in evaluating the moral status of certain theistic views apart from the background beliefs that motivate them. Whether opposition to abortion is immoral, for example, cannot be assessed apart from a consideration of the relevant philosophical and theological beliefs of those who oppose it—in this case, beliefs about what constitutes a human person. Harris contends that, in general, conservative Christians are not much concerned about human suffering—that they are obsessed, instead, with concerns about what human activities God might find offensive.[2] But this ignores the conservative Christian beliefs that the highest good for a human being is eternal communion with God, and that anything which jeopardizes a person's relationship with God thereby jeopardizes—among other things—that person's ultimate happiness. Thus, Christians are not unconcerned with human suffering; they simply hold different views than the atheist about what kinds of human suffering (and happiness) are at stake and what ways one can act to combat (or promote) them.

Such pragmatic arguments against theistic belief, then, should be judged unconvincing. We do not mean to imply by this that it is uncommon—or even inappropriate—to take into account the practical fruits of a certain belief system in assessing its veracity. There is no doubt that many people have been turned away from religious beliefs by what they see as bad behavior by believers, just as many people have been drawn to religious belief by the lives of saintly people. Particular individuals may find reasons of this kind personally compelling. But we see little hope that such pragmatic arguments can be made into a compelling proof that would command general assent. In the remainder of this chapter we will focus instead on the question of whether religious commitments are *reasonable*, in the sense of rationally defensible, addressing the question first in general terms and then with reference to the plurality of world religions, with their competing truth claims.

Faith: Subjectivity in Religious Arguments

The student who enters the critical dialogue we have called philosophy of religion may initially hope that rational reflection will eliminate the pluralism of competing perspectives. But such a hope seems doomed to disappointment. It appears, rather, that the disagreements that are present among people in general reappear among philosophers.

Why does such disagreement continue to exist? Doubtless, there are many reasons. An important one, which we will explore later, is that religious beliefs impinge directly on the way a person should live. To accept or reject a religion is to accept or reject a whole way of life, and such decisions involve the emotions as much as the intellect. It is not surprising that people who do not want to live as Christians, and who want Christianity to be false, find certain arguments compelling, which justify their unbelief.

A second reason for disagreement among philosophers of religion has to do with the subjective commitments, the gut convictions, which philosophers, as human beings, bring to their analyses of the arguments. In our examination of the arguments for and against religious belief, we stumbled on this factor again and again. Ultimately, whether an argument is sound depends not just on its validity but also on the truth of its premises. In many cases a key premise is judged reasonable or plausible by one individual, while another finds that premise doubtful at best.

The ontological argument, for example, seems sound if it is granted that God's existence is possible. The cosmological argument will be judged sound if one accepts the principle of sufficient reason, especially if one interprets the experience of cosmic wonder as evidence of the contingency of the natural world. The teleological argument will be judged sound if one interprets certain phenomena in the natural world as examples of beneficial order. The moral argument will be judged convincing if certain views about the nature of morality are accepted.

On the other side, the argument from evil against God's existence requires one to judge whether one knows any evil in the world to be utterly pointless, or whether one's grounds for believing in its pointlessness are superior to one's grounds for believing in a good God. Similar comments could be made about the arguments concerning the possibility of miracles, revelation claims and the analysis of religious experience.

In looking at the "objective" arguments, pro and con, it seems that we are continually thrust back to personal, subjective judgments—to that moment when an individual judges a certain claim simply to have "the ring of truth." As a result, some have concluded that such rational reflection is of little value. In the end, doesn't it all boil down to a leap of faith: a blind decision, unsupported by reason?

We must begin by noting that if one wishes to speak of leaps of faith, the religious believer is not the only one who does the leaping. The basic convictions that shape the conclusions of the atheist in these matters are equally subjective. Atheism can no more be proved by valid arguments with uncontroversially true premises than can theism. As it turns out, however, the leap-of-faith metaphor is misleading in several respects. The metaphor conjures up an image of a person who makes an arbitrary choice to believe or not to believe. But it does not seem possible, in normal cases, to simply *decide* to believe something. We can believe only what seems true to us, because to believe something is to think that it *is* true (or at least *likely* true). No matter how hard one tries, one cannot simply adopt by a sheer act of will the belief that HIV/AIDS does not exist, regardless of how comforting such a belief might be.

It is true that faith plays a key role in the judgments we ultimately make about religious questions. But what the leap-of-faith image misses is that the faith which is crucial is not, for the most part, a kind of faith that a person can simply manufacture by a momentary act of will. The faith that shapes the individual's judgments is, rather, a faith the individual already possesses. This faith consists of the basic convictions, attitudes and values that the person *brings to* her reflection on the viability of theism.

This faith, of course, is not unalterable. It can be developed and changed. Both rational reflection and moments of decision play important roles in the process of developing or altering faith. But if one is to talk of faith in connection with the judgments one makes about religious matters, it is crucial to see this faith as a set of long-term qualities of whole persons, not as a momentary act of the will.

The Evidentialist Challenge to Religious Belief

The existence of contrasting faiths in different people accounts for a good number of the disagreements among religions. It troubles many people that faith plays such a crucial role in religious judgments. Even if faith is not seen as an arbitrary, blind leap, it still seems to undermine the claims of religious believers to *know* religious truths.

Lurking behind this anxiety is the strong foundationalist epistemology we in chapter one termed "neutralism." It seems to many people that if someone's judgment that a set of religious beliefs is true is partly grounded in faith convictions which are not shared by everyone, then such a judgment cannot be objectively certain. Is commitment reasonable in such a case? Can such a belief amount to knowledge?

These questions raise fundamental epistemological issues about the nature of knowledge and justification. A full treatment of them would require a fully worked-out epistemology.[3] Here we can do no more than sketch the perspective on them which seems most reasonable.

Recall that the classical foundationalist ideal in epistemology is "objective certainty": it seems to the foundationalist that our knowledge must be based on a foundation that is so certain as to be acceptable to any sane, reasonable person. A reasonable person—according to the foundationalist's assessment—is one who avoids commitment in cases where the commitment cannot be objectively guaranteed, verified or proven. It seems to follow that reason and faith are mutually hostile. Someone who relies on personal faith commitments is being unreasonable, because reason demands that an individual put aside all prejudices, preconceptions and presuppositions.

This foundationalist ideal takes many forms. In its *empiricist* form it demands that we rely solely on empirically verifiable facts in determining our beliefs. In its *rationalist* form it asks that we begin with basic premises which are self-evident to reason. In all its classical forms foundationalism is an attempt to eliminate subjectivity—and risk—from the knowing process. To use John Dewey's phrase, it is "a quest for certainty"; it wants, however, not merely certainty but an objective certainty in which the individual makes no risky commitments as an individual.

In the nineteenth century this risk-averse approach to knowledge was taken by W. K. Clifford, who argued that it is not only intellectually dishonest but downright immoral to believe anything beyond what is adequately supported by evidence. To illustrate why he thinks this, Clifford imagines a ship owner who has doubts about whether the vessel he is about to send out, filled with emigrants, is in fact seaworthy, but who stifles these doubts and manages to convince himself—apart from any evidence to support it—that the ship will certainly reach its destination safely. What should we say of this man when the ship subsequently goes down, drowning all aboard? Clifford argues that the man should be judged guilty of the deaths of the passengers: "It is admitted that he did sincerely believe in the soundness of the ship; but the sincerity of his conviction can in nowise help him, because *he had no right to believe on such evidence as was before him*."[4] This judgment, Clifford thinks, can be generalized: he claims, (in)famously, that "it is wrong always, everywhere, and for any one, to believe anything upon insufficient evidence."[5]

Clifford's thesis is a rather extreme version of a view called *evidentialism*. His argument is typically understood as an attack on religious belief, which Clifford seems to presume is not supported sufficiently by evidence—at least, not the kind of evidence that Clifford has in mind. Given that believers cannot prove that God exists, either by an uncontroversially sound proof or by direct sensory verification that is available to everyone, their belief in God is irrational, even immoral. Let us call this the *evidentialist challenge to religious belief*.

In Clifford's unrestricted form, evidentialism is wildly implausible: it is easy to come up with scenarios in which an individual surely is not immoral for holding a certain unfounded belief, even if that individual is in some way violating some rational or epistemic standard. (Imagine someone who believes, for no good reason, that he has exactly ten thousand hairs on his head.) Yet Clifford's thesis, with all its unrestricted quantifiers ("always," "everywhere," "any one," "anything"), cannot admit even a single exception. Most evidentialists today hold a more modest view, omitting the ethical judgment and holding instead that beliefs are rationally *unjustified* if they are not supported by sufficient evidence. The indictment of religious belief, however, remains at the forefront of many evidentialists' agendas. Sam Harris, for example, caustically laments, "While believing strongly, without evidence, is considered a mark of madness or stupidity in any other area of our lives, faith in God still holds immense prestige in our society."[6]

Reformed Epistemology

How should the theist respond to the evidentialist challenge? Apart from concession, two general types of responses are possible. First, the theist can grant the evidentialist's claim that beliefs are justified only if supported by sufficient evidence, but then go on to argue that religious beliefs are, in fact, sufficiently supported. If this route is taken, the theist will likely begin by challenging the assumption that evidence is "sufficient" to support a belief only if it renders that belief "incorrigible" ("impossible of being mistaken"), pointing out that this assumption has absurd consequences. (Even the most mundane beliefs—for example, the belief that one is now reading a book—fail to meet this standard.) She will then proceed to clarify the notion of evidence, arguing that it is not limited to what we can perceive through our five senses, but extends also to the rational support that can be provided by, for example, philosophical arguments. The stage is then set for the theist to try to marshal the resources of natural theology, religious experience, special revelation and so on to produce sufficient evidence to justify religious belief.

Many theists—some of whom are themselves evidentialists—have adopted this kind of response to the evidentialist challenge. But another strategy is available. Rather than trying to show that religious belief enjoys evidential support, one can instead challenge the assumption that beliefs require the support of evidence to be rationally justified. Alvin Plantinga has developed at length this line of response to evidentialism.[7] Plantinga's approach is called *Reformed epistemology:* it follows in the tradition of the Protestant Reformer and theologian John Calvin in its view that belief in God can be rationally justified apart from any arguments or evidence because it is (or can be) *properly basic.* A belief is *basic* for a person if he does not hold it on the basis of other beliefs that he holds; it is *properly* basic if it is also rationally justified for him, despite this lack of support from other beliefs.

Plantinga's view immediately raises two questions. First, why think that any beliefs are properly basic? Second, even if there are some properly basic beliefs, why think that belief in God is among them? We will address these in order.

To see why Plantinga thinks some beliefs are properly basic, we must return to our discussion of foundationalism, which is the approach to knowledge that underlies and motivates the evidentialist challenge. As we noted earlier, the classical foundationalist regards objective certainty as the epistemic ideal. Rationally justified beliefs are those that are supported, ultimately, by foundational beliefs which are themselves absolutely certain or "indubitable," as Descartes puts it. It is necessary, however, for these foundational beliefs to be properly basic; otherwise, we face a problem of infinite regress. An evidential relation is a relation among beliefs: it is a relation that holds when one belief provides rational support for another belief. But if every belief requires other beliefs to support it, then we are headed for an infinite regress of justifying beliefs, which seems to imply that ultimately no belief can be rationally justified. But this is absurd; surely many of our beliefs *are* justified. Therefore, there must be some properly basic beliefs.

But why think that belief in God might be among this set of foundational, properly basic beliefs? The kinds of beliefs typically taken to be foundational include beliefs in self-evident, necessary truths (e.g., that 2 + 2 = 4), incorrigible beliefs (e.g., that one presently exists or that one is presently in pain) and beliefs about what is "evident to the senses" (e.g., that one is now holding a book). But as Plantinga points out, if foundationalism stipulates that properly basic beliefs are restricted to just beliefs of these three kinds, it will end up being self-defeating.[8]

To see this, consider the following claim: for any proposition *p*, a belief *p* is properly basic only if *p* is either self-evident or incorrigible or evident to the senses. Call this claim F. The problem, in short, is that F is neither self-evident nor incorrigible nor evident to the senses. Thus, belief in F is not properly basic. It follows that one is justified in believing F only if it is supported by other beliefs that *are* properly basic: that is, other beliefs that are self-evident or incorrigible or evident to the senses. But it seems unlikely that F is supported by any such beliefs. If it is not, then no one is justified in believing F, the cornerstone proposition of the kind of foundationalism we have described. It follows that foundationalism, thus construed, is self-defeating: no one can be justified in believing it.

To circumvent this problem the foundationalist must broaden the scope of what qualifies as a properly basic belief, such that the statement of what qualifies will meet its own criteria for being a proposition that one could be rationally justified in believing. (Besides the problem of being self-defeating, F is obviously too restrictive for another reason: it implies that a large portion of our ordinary beliefs are unjustified—for example, our ordinary memory beliefs, such as a belief that one had cereal for breakfast—on the grounds that they are neither self-evident nor incorrigible nor evident to the senses.) It is clear then that the foundationalist must be more lenient about what kinds of beliefs qualify as properly basic. This is just the foothold that Plantinga needs; he now raises the question: why couldn't it be that, as Calvin and other Reformed thinkers claimed, belief in God is among those beliefs that qualify as properly basic?[9] In order for the evidentialist objection to be successful, Plantinga argues, its proponents "must specify a criterion for proper basicality that is free from self-referential difficulties, rules out belief in God as properly basic, and is such that there is some reason to think it is true."[10] As of yet, no one has been able to do this, and thus the evidentialist objection to religious belief fails.

As developed so far, Plantinga's response might strike some readers as being rather glib—and perhaps even fallacious. Even if Plantinga is right that no evidentialist has been able to specify a criterion for proper basicality that rules out belief in God, this by itself gives us no reason to think that belief in God really is properly basic. To think otherwise is to commit the fallacy of *appeal to ignorance* ("It has not been proved that *p* is false; therefore, *p* is true"). This response, however, misconstrues Plantinga's argument, which aims to show only that the evidentialist argument is unsound, not to prove that belief in God is, in fact, properly basic. The evidentialist objector has brought the charge of irrationality against the theist, and it is up to the objector to make the case for this accusation. Plantinga has simply shown that the case against theism presented by the evidentialist is flawed. His argument, then, is not fallacious.

Nor is his response glib. There are positive reasons for thinking that belief in God ranks among those beliefs that are properly basic; the view is in fact a part of the Reformed tradition from the beginning. Calvin held that God has created us with a *sensus divinitatis* (sense of the divine): an innate tendency or disposition to form an immediate (noninferential) belief in God. Calvin writes,

> "There is within the human mind, and indeed by natural instinct, an awareness of divinity." This we take to be beyond controversy. To prevent anyone from taking refuge in the pretense of ignorance, God himself has implanted in all men a certain understanding of divine majesty. . . . So deeply does the common conception occupy the minds of all, so tenaciously does it inhere in the hearts of all! Therefore, since from the beginning of the world there has been no region, no city, in short, no household, that could do without religion, there lies in this a tacit confession of a sense of deity inscribed in the hearts of all.
>
> Indeed, the perversity of the impious, who though they struggle furiously are unable to extricate themselves from the fear of God, is abundant testimony that this conviction, namely, that *there is some God*, is naturally inborn in all, and is fixed deep within, as it were in the very marrow.[11]

On Calvin's view, then, the *sensus divinitatis* provides an explanation for why belief in God is so pervasive. The explanation for why some resist belief in God, nonetheless, is that human beings are sinful. In the unnatural condition in which we have existed since the Fall, our natural tendency to believe in God can be—and often is—suppressed. This is, perhaps first and foremost, among the *noetic effects of sin:* the pernicious and corrupting effects of sin on the mind. Nevertheless, the disposition to belief is present in everyone, and it is "triggered" by common experiences: Calvin notes especially the experience of marveling at "the workmanship of the universe," but we could add to this the experience of "hearing" God's speaking to oneself when listening to a powerful sermon or reading the Bible, or the experience of feeling that God disapproves of one's actions upon doing something that one knows is wrong—and many other such common experiences as well.[12] According to Calvin such experiences provide occasions for the formation of justified beliefs in God's existence; in fact, Calvin thinks, they even provide one with *knowledge* that God exists.

Plantinga's case for justified religious belief is not yet complete. He goes on to answer prominent objections, including (1) the worry that if belief in God is properly basic, then *any* belief can qualify as properly basic ("the Great Pumpkin objection"), (2) the objection that Plantinga himself offers no alternative, positive criterion of proper basicality, (3) the objection that belief in God is *groundless* if it is basic, (4) the objection that those who take belief in God as basic will hold this belief "come what may," that is, regardless of any counterevidence they are presented with and (5) the objection that his view reduces to fideism.[13] We will not rehearse these objections—or Plantinga's responses to them—here; the interested reader is advised to consult Plantinga's now-classic essay "Reason and Belief in God," which is accessible even to the beginning student of philosophy of religion.

The Place of Subjectivity in Forming Beliefs

Our discussion so far strongly suggests that the evidentialist challenge to religious belief can be squarely met. Even apart from our efforts to meet the evidentialist challenge, however, there are good reasons to conclude that the classical foundationalist approach to knowledge is flawed. Contrary to the wishes of such foundationalists, it seems clear that the overwhelming majority of our everyday beliefs rest on interpretive judgments that incorporate a personal element. The ideal of objective certainty, in the foundationalist sense, turns out to be, for the most part, a pipedream. In everyday life, individuals make countless judgments which they regard as reasonable but which do not attain the standards of the classical foundationalist ideal.

In fact, the risk-free approach advocated by Clifford—refraining from forming any belief wherever there is insufficient evidence to decide the matter—comes at a high price: as William James points out, there are circumstances in which adopting this attitude will put the attainment of truth beyond reach.[14] There may be truths in which, as James puts it, *"faith in a fact can help create the fact."*[15]

Suppose, for example, that one adopted the policy of refusing to believe that one was liked by any person until that person *proved* it by his actions. Chances are that such an attitude of suspicion would be off-putting to others. As a result it is likely that one will not be, in general, well-liked by many people. Faith in a fact ("Other people like me") can help create the fact. James's example is a particularly apt one for religious knowledge, since interpersonal knowledge among humans shares many features of religious knowledge. But we can imagine other scenarios as well: consider recent medical studies indicating that those who believe that they will fully recover after some major surgery are statistically more likely to actually experience a full recovery. Clifford's principle—which in this case would lead one to judge that such patients are actually *immoral* for believing, in the absence of evidence, that they will recover fully—is, in James's assessment, an "insane logic." James concludes,

> I therefore, for one, cannot see my way to accepting the agnostic rules for truth-seeking, or wilfully agree to keep my willing nature out of the game. I cannot do so for this plain reason,

> that *a rule of thinking which would absolutely prevent me from acknowledging certain kinds of truth if those kinds of truth were really there, would be an irrational rule.*[16]

The relevance of James's view to religious belief is obvious. Perhaps it is the case that the Christian gospel is the sort of truth which requires an initial leap of faith to accept, and perhaps this initial act of faith is one which initiates a relationship with God that ultimately results in an experience of God's love that confirms the truth of what one believes. Such is the way many have viewed Christianity.

James's argument, however, is intended not as an argument for Christianity but rather to advance the general point that those, like Clifford, who think they can avoid risk by adopting a hard-nosed, "scientific," evidentialist criterion of belief are mistaken. Those who adopt Clifford's principle avoid one kind of risk—namely, the possibility of adopting false beliefs—only by incurring another—namely, the possibility of losing out on gaining the truth. One is within one's epistemic rights to adopt this kind of approach, if one so chooses—James does not wish to deny this—but the point is that reason does not demand it. To adopt Clifford's principle is, in its own way, to exercise faith: faith that any possible truth that is lost thereby is outweighed by the good of the false beliefs it helps one to avoid. Faith—and the risk that attends it—is unavoidable for finite, epistemically limited human beings.

It is interesting to note that (as was briefly discussed in chapter one) philosophers of science such as Thomas Kuhn and Stephen Toulmin have argued that faith commitments play a positive role even in the sciences.[17] In becoming a scientist an individual becomes a part of a scientific community, which is defined by the shared values, attitudes and basic assumptions of its members. These shared commitments are embodied not only in theories but in the life and practice of the community, and they are acquired not only through overt instruction but by the individual's coming to share in that communal form of life.

The classical foundationalist ideal of objective certainty does not seem, then, to be either realistic or desirable, even in areas of life other than religion. There seems little reason, therefore, to impose it on religion, where, it would seem, faith surely has a legitimate role to play in human life, if it has such a role anywhere.

Interpretive Judgments and the Nature of a "Cumulative Case"

With the abandonment of the classical foundationalist ideal—which we have seen to collapse on a number of different fronts—the way seems open for developing a view of reason that will make it possible to see faith and reason as potential allies, instead of competitors. Before trying to construct this view, however, let us first consider why foundationalism initially appears attractive to many people. The motivating reason seems to be, first and foremost, the fear that abandoning the ideal of objective certainty will open the floodgates to superstition and nonsense. The choice foundationalists see is one between objective certainty and a blind leap of faith, the latter meaning that "anything goes."

One way of looking at the foundationalist ideal is as a quest for an "algorithm" to decide religious questions. An algorithm is a decision procedure in mathematics which, when followed correctly, is guaranteed to lead to a solution of a problem. A procedure with a finite number of steps, capable of being followed by anyone, is the ideal. We might question whether a religious algorithm would even be desirable. For present purposes, however, what must be attacked head-on is this false disjunction: *either* an algorithm *or* an irrational leap. There is a great deal of room between these two extremes, and reasonable judgments can be made in a great many areas of human life where algorithmic decision procedures are lacking. A key element in such areas is the concept of an "interpretive judgment."

In *The Justification of Religious Belief*, Basil Mitchell gives several examples of reason at work in nonalgorithmic areas.[18] One is the area of historical scholarship. Historians often disagree about the causes of a particular event or its meaning. Though rival historians may agree on many facts, they often disagree about how these facts should be interpreted and their significance evaluated.

Another excellent example is the field of literary criticism. Literary scholars often disagree about the meaning of a poem. Is a particular line to be regarded as irony, satire or straightforward praise?

In both of these areas, "objective" factors play an important role. Rival historians search for facts that will support their own theories, and they interpret the facts in accordance with their overall theory. Rival critics look for features of the poem which support their interpretation, as well as other sorts of data, such as known facts about the author's attitudes. Such disagreements may not, in the end, be objectively resolvable to the satisfaction of all parties. However, this does not mean that reason has no role to play in such matters. We can still distinguish between interpretations that are reasonable and those that are preposterous. In recognizing the role of interpretation and the lack of an algorithm, the floodgates to nonsense have not by any means been thrown open.

These examples are instructive in philosophy of religion, for *interpretation* will play a key role in defending or attacking religious beliefs as well. The proponent of the cosmological argument interprets the experience of cosmic wonder differently than her opponent. The proponent of the moral argument interprets morality differently than does his opponent. The religious individual who perceives God *through* a sermon, song or religious text interprets her experience very differently than does the nonreligious person.

Indeed, it is very likely that the experiences themselves differ. For in speaking of interpretation we do not mean to refer only, or even mainly, to a consciously articulated process that follows experience, but also to those interpretive features that are already present in experience. We do not usually *simply* see or hear; we see something *as* something and hear something *as* something.

One feature of interpretation that calls for special attention is the way interpretive judgments presuppose one another. This feature is often referred to as *the hermeneutic circle,* for it seems that interpretive or hermeneutical arguments are circular. One's reading of the individual parts of a text, for example, is strongly influenced by one's overall view of the text's main thrust. Yet how does one acquire an understanding of that whole apart from an understanding of the parts?

This circle is resolved by each of us when we read a book or poem. How do we do it? Initially, we simply plunge in and start reading, relying on what might be termed our "preunderstanding." Drawing on any background knowledge we may have and our overall experience and judgment, we begin where we are, and we form an overall impression of what the piece is all about, one that provides us with a perspective from which to interpret as we read further. This initial hypothesis is not, however, carved in stone. It is modified and reshaped as it is put to the test of making sense of the individual text. This "testing process" becomes even more in evidence as the individual encounters and considers rival readings.

When would we say that such an interpretive judgment is reasonable? Not, we submit, when it is the result of a presuppositionless, neutral standpoint, for such a "neutral" reader could not even begin to read the piece in question. Rather, *an interpretive judgment is reasonable when it can survive the process of critical testing.* A reasonable interpretation is one which accounts for the facts, suggests new insights, illuminates meaningful patterns—and does so better than its rivals. In this process the subjective preferences that the individual brings to the process are more than an unavoidable nuisance; they are part of what makes the whole business possible.

When tested, these subjective preferences cease to be merely subjective preferences. For the criteria used in testing them are *not* arbitrary but are implicitly recognized as valid by all parties to the controversy. These criteria are factors such as the following: (1) *Logical consistency.* Does the system of beliefs contradict itself? (2) *Coherence.* Coherence is more than bare logical consistency, which is simply the absence of contradiction. Coherence is a positive harmony, a fitting together of beliefs into an organic whole. (3) *Factual adequacy.* Does the belief system account for all the facts? How well does it do so? (4) *Intellectual fertility.* Does a belief system give rise to new discoveries and insights, suggest new illuminating patterns, call one's attention to unnoticed dimensions of experience?

The case for or against a set of religious beliefs will necessarily appeal to those kinds of criteria. Because such criteria often have to be applied to a belief system as a whole, it seems that the justification for a set of religious beliefs is unlikely to consist of a single, linear argument, but of what Basil Mitchell has called a *cumulative case.*

Mitchell uses as an illustration for a cumulative case a hypothetical case of two explorers who stumble on a large depression in the ground.[19] One takes the hole to be the result of purposeful intelligence; the other does not. Somewhat later, they discover other similar depressions. The first person thinks he sees a pattern in the relations between the holes; to the other party, they are just ordinary holes. Later still, they find in a cave some manuscripts, faint and obscure. The first explorer excitedly claims to have a document that in some way shows the design and function of the holes. To the second party, the document is cryptic, and it is not clear that it has anything to do with the holes in question.

Mitchell means his story to be a parable of the argument between the religious believer and the unbeliever. The large hole corresponds to the experience of finitude and contingency that generates the cosmological argument. The smaller holes correspond to the considerations that fuel such arguments as the teleological and moral arguments, as well as the evidence from religious experience. The documents found in the cave correspond to alleged special revelations, in which God has perhaps spelled out the meaning of things in more detail. The case the believer wants to make will not be based on any one of these factors taken in isolation. Each individual piece of evidence involves an element of interpretation, and the force of the overall case depends both on its ability to account for each part and on its ability to show meaningful, coherent patterns among the parts.

Thus, the theist finds it strange that there should be a contingent universe, and wonders why it exists. He finds it stranger still that the universe should show abundant examples of beneficial order and that it should seem to contain a moral as well as a physical order. When he adds to these considerations the mass of religious experiences in which people claim to be aware of God, theism becomes, at the very least, a plausible hypothesis, a reasonable interpretation of experience. Confronted by a well-attested special revelation, which was accompanied by miracles and which provides insight into his own life, giving him a deep understanding of his basic failures and genuine needs, such a person might very reasonably become an adherent of a living religion.

The atheist can, of course, mount a cumulative case as well. But her case will be equally interpretive in nature. In both cases there is no reason for the individual to consign the whole matter of religious belief to the limbo of irrationalism. For such cases can be critically tested and reasonable judgments made about them. There is, perhaps, even less likelihood that total agreement will be reached in religion than in areas like literary criticism, for reasons we will soon discuss. But a judgment that reflects the personal *faith* of the one judging can still be a reasonable judgment, provided the individual is willing to put his convictions to the test.

Can Faith Be Certain?

Let us assume that a cumulative case, relying at certain points on interpretive judgments, can be constructed for a set of religious beliefs. Such a case would provide a rational basis for belief, if one is willing to admit the existence of a nonalgorithmic type of rationality. A skeptic might still object at this point that such a case could never really justify a genuine religious faith. One of the marks of a genuine religious commitment is that such commitments have an unconditional, decisive character. Such commitments are total commitments. But the evidence underlying religious belief falls short of being conclusive, which is what would be needed to justify absolute certainty. To the skeptic this means that a reasonable commitment to religious belief must always be tentative in nature. In support of this, he could cite our own contention, in the previous section, that an openness to critical testing and revision in the light of new evidence is essential if a faith commitment is to be reasonable.

The skeptic's view at this point presupposes what some have called an *ethics of belief.* Though we have not introduced the term before now, we have encountered this idea before, in our discussion of Clifford. In this case the ethical principle seems to be that firmness of belief ought always to be proportionate to the quality of the evidence for the belief. (Let us call this the *proportionality principle.*) Even if we admit the reasonableness of belief on the basis of evidence that is less than algorithmic, surely the degree of belief ought to reflect the degree of evidence, says the skeptic.

To respond to the skeptic's charge here, we must give a more careful analysis of the nature of religious belief, and of the nature of belief generally. H. H. Price, in his classic study *Belief,* distinguishes two major types of theories of belief.[20] According to one view, which we shall call *the mental-assent view,* a belief is a mental act, an occurrence in which the mind considers a proposition and performs the act of assenting to it. According to the second theory, which we might call *the behavioral-disposition theory,* a belief is a tendency or disposition to act or behave in certain ways, under certain conditions. Thus, if one believes that one resides in the state of Minnesota, that does not mean that one is continually, consciously, considering that proposition. Rather, the belief consists in hypothetical or dispositional facts about one's behavior, such as these: if one is asked what state one resides in, one will reply, "Minnesota"; if one books a round-trip flight, the city of the initial departure and final destination will be in Minnesota and so forth.

Price concludes that neither view is completely adequate by itself. The mental-assent view does not recognize the way in which beliefs express themselves in action, and it cannot explain the fact that one continues to believe things of which one is not at the moment consciously thinking. The behavioral-disposition view ignores the reality of mental acts of assent and has difficulty specifying in a noncircular way what acts and dispositions a belief consists in. Ultimately, a proponent of this view is forced to say that a person who believes proposition *p* will perform those acts that a person who believes *p* will perform. Price concludes that a combined theory is best—a theory that recognizes the "dispositional" character of belief, but regards beliefs as consisting not merely in being disposed to perform overt actions but also to perform those mental acts of belief which Price terms "assentings."

Price's conclusion provides a good starting place for understanding religious belief as well. True religious belief cannot be reduced simply to behaving in a certain way. To believe that God is worthy of worship is not *simply* to perform acts of worship. Rather, the religious believer worships God *because* he believes that God is worthy of worship. He mentally assents to propositions like "God is real," "God is holy" and "God wants me to love and obey him." On the other hand, genuine religious belief clearly does not consist merely in mental acts of assent either. In the Christian religion, for example, true faith must make a difference to the believer's life. "Faith without works is dead," says the apostle James, and merely to assent to God's existence is to do no more than the devils, who also give intellectual assent to this (Jas 2:14-26).

It is not that the religious believer does not assent to certain propositions. Rather, it is that, in virtue of the very nature of those propositions, the person who merely assents to them intellectually thereby shows that, in one important sense, he does not believe them. Religious beliefs, even more than beliefs generally, have an essentially *prescriptive* role. Their very being, one might say, consists in their being more than mere intellectual assent. If they are genuine, they express themselves in action.

This characteristic of religious beliefs has significant implications for the problem posed by the proportionality principle, which is advocated by some as part of the ethics of belief. If religious beliefs consisted solely of mental acts of assent, then it would make sense to say that such beliefs should be proportionate to the evidence and therefore that such beliefs should not possess an "unconditional" character unless the evidence supporting them were absolutely conclusive. If religious beliefs consist mainly of dispositions to perform certain actions, however, and if the religious propositions to which one mentally assents have prescriptive implications for one's total life, then the proportionality principle may not be correct. The reason for this is that many actions do not admit of degrees; they have an absolute character, in the sense that one either does the action or does not. But surely it is too much to demand of all such actions that their reasonableness be demonstrable by evidence that is absolutely conclusive.

Furthermore, many actions, if done at all, must be done in an enthusiastic, wholehearted manner. Suppose a person suffering from depression is considering some kind of behavioral therapy. If she actually embarks on a program of therapy, it is reasonable for her to give it her best shot and participate wholeheartedly in the program, even if she has no proof it will help her. She knows that a timid, halfhearted commitment will not give the program of therapy a fair trial. In a sense, a wholehearted commitment, far from precluding an honest test of a risky commitment, is sometimes a condition for such a test.

An even clearer illustration might be the choice to marry. A woman who is considering offers of marriage from different men has no algorithm for determining which choice is "right" for her. If she decides to marry, however, it would be the height of foolishness to refrain from committing herself wholeheartedly to the marriage on the grounds that her evidence that the marriage will be successful is less than conclusive.

The case of religious faith seems to be similar. In Christianity, for example, Jesus confronts potential followers with certain claims and demands on them. Claiming to be the Son of God, he demands a willingness to sacrifice any and every finite good for him. He demanded that the rich young ruler give away all his goods and come and follow him (Lk 18:18-23). The rich young ruler had to decide whether he really believed Jesus had the authority to make such a request, and, if so, whether he wished to obey. Imagine another rich young ruler who was willing to obey if he were convinced that Jesus was truly the Messiah. Suppose he reviewed the evidence, pro and con, and decided he had good reason to believe. If he then believed in Jesus, he ought, at that point, to be willing to stake everything on Jesus' words. It would not be reasonable for him to decide to give away a little of his wealth on the grounds that he did not have absolute proof that Jesus was truly the Messiah. Such partial obedience would still be disobedience.

Furthermore, since most religions make predictions about the deepest experiences of believers, a wholehearted commitment may make it possible to test some of the claims of the religion in a unique way, just as a wholehearted commitment to a program of therapy is an essential condition for testing the effectiveness of the program. If the rich young ruler had decided to follow Jesus, the outcome would have been significant. Would the young man by that action have gained a sense of inner peace, an understanding of what life is all about, a sense of forgiveness for his own past failures? Perhaps a halfhearted, wavering faith would not have provided a significant test of the claims of Christianity to provide these things.

In summary, it is the nature of true religious belief that it be part of a way of life. Committing oneself to such a way of life seems to be the sort of thing that must be done in an all-or-nothing, unconditional manner, if it is to be done at all, even if the evidence for the commitment is a matter of degree.

This fact squares well with some other, widely recognized features of religious faith. One is that religious faith is not completely or even largely a product of rational calculation. Christians, for example, insist that genuine faith is a response to what God has done for an individual, that it is not something a person can simply develop on his own. This makes sense if faith is viewed as a total way of life and not merely as a series of acts of mental assent. The passion that fuels such a life commitment and gives it an unconditional character is no mere intellectual belief, and it is not just the result of the reviewing of evidence. Conversely, the person who rejects religious faith also does so on grounds which are not merely rational. If religious faith makes claims on our total life, it is not surprising that many should find those claims burdensome and that this may color the way such people view the evidence. This helps to explain the continuing lack of agreement about religious matters among both ordinary people and critical philosophers. But to say that faith or its lack is not merely the product of rational reflection does not imply that a person cannot reflect on the reasonableness of such a commitment, nor that such reflection is unimportant.

Our argument that it may be reasonable to decisively hold a belief for which there is good but not absolutely compelling evidence does not, of course, imply that all religious beliefs must be held in this unconditional manner. Most religious believers do hold some of their beliefs in a tentative manner, recognizing them as less central to their faith than others. A Christian's belief that she has been redeemed by Jesus' life, death and resurrection may be held more firmly than any particular theory as to how this atonement was accomplished, for example.

Faith and Doubt: Can Religious Faith Be Tested?

If one admits that a faith based on less-than-conclusive evidence can nonetheless reasonably be "total" or decisive in character, then the opposite problem might seem to appear. Earlier, we argued that a reasonable faith must be open to initial testing. But can a person who is wholeheartedly committed to a faith genuinely and honestly evaluate that faith?

It may seem that to test one's belief, one would have to be able to doubt it; and doubt seems incompatible with robust faith. But there are different kinds of doubt. Let us distinguish *logical doubt* from *existential doubt*. Logical doubt is a willingness to imaginatively consider the possibility that one's own convictions are mistaken by honestly considering the new evidence and comparing one's case with other possible cumulative cases. Existential doubt is a genuine worry that one's own position is seriously flawed or that it is quite possibly wrong.

A certain amount of existential doubt seems acceptable and even normal in a religious life. The great saints are, in many cases, not people who were always free of doubt, but rather people who were able to deal with their doubts and act decisively in spite of them.[21] A person willing to sacrifice her life for her faith would by no means have a faith which is somehow inferior or less than decisive, even if that person at times struggled with existential doubt. We must remember that religious beliefs are primarily dispositions to action. The test as to whether a person is truly a believer is not whether the person always mentally assents in a doubt-free manner to religious propositions. The true test is whether the person is willing to *act* on those beliefs.

It seems clear then that a certain amount of existential doubt can coexist with strong religious faith. If existential doubt becomes too great or too frequent, however, faith might be crippled or cease to exist altogether. But whatever tension may be present between faith and existential doubt, there is no necessary tension between faith and logical doubt. Inherent in one's belief that things are a particular way is an understanding of how things could be different. If one is genuinely convinced that one's belief is true, one will not shrink from examining rival views. To the degree that one is certain and confident, one will welcome testing. A faith that evades critical questions is a faith that lacks confidence, a faith that is *not* truly assured it has found truth. Paradoxical as it may sound, confidence in one's convictions may make it possible to put those convictions to serious test. A recognition of the logical possibility that one could be mistaken is not a reason to believe that one actually is mistaken. Similarly, an imaginative ability to empathize with a rival position, so as to compare it with one's own, does not mean that one is actually doubting one's beliefs existentially.

This is not to say that religious believers will or should continually seek out objections to their faith. Belief is, after all, to be lived. If we spent all our time critically reflecting on our faith, we would have no time to live out that faith. And religious faith is tested in part by the very process of living it out. Nevertheless, it is appropriate for religious believers, as they have the intellectual ability and opportunity, to spend some time reflecting on their faith and its reasonableness.

One final point: Much of the preceding discussion has worked from the implicit assumption that reasonable faith must be based, in part at least, on evidence. If the Reformed epistemologists are right, and certain faith beliefs are properly basic, matters will be somewhat different. However, even properly basic beliefs can be undermined by "defeaters," and thus even a Reformed epistemologist can recognize the importance of critical testing and evaluating evidence.

What Is Faith?

In the preceding discussion, the term "faith" has been used in a variety of senses. We have used the term to refer to the assumptions, convictions and attitudes which the believer *brings to* a consideration of the evidence for and against religious truth. We have also used the term to refer to the commitment that is, in some cases, the *outcome* of this reflection. We have used "faith" to refer to the subjective preferences of people generally, and to refer to the specific kind of commitment which is involved in being a Christian. What, then, is faith?

Faith is all of these, though this must not be taken to imply that there are no significant differences between the various kinds of faith. In a sense every person has "faith"; everyone has deep-rooted assumptions, convictions and attitudes that color what counts as evidence for him and how that evidence is interpreted. This is the kind of faith one brings to the evidence. Insofar as beliefs are reflected in action, and people must make choices, everyone also has faith in the sense of commitments, which may or may not be informed by rational reflection.

In the ongoing life of an actual person, these are simply two different moments in what might be called the faith dimension of life. The faith which we bring to our reflection embodies previous commitments, and the commitment which is the outcome of reflection is the faith which we bring to our future reflection. Faith can legitimately be thought of as both prior conviction and commitment. Yet this movement—from prior conviction through rational reflection and on to commitment—cannot be understood as simply a series of sequential events, for the having of convictions, the reflecting and the committing interpenetrate each other in the most complex fashion.

This general structure of faith—as the personal commitment which both informs reflection and is shaped by reflection—is common to both the religious believer and nonbeliever. Both have faith in both of these senses. This does not, however, imply that religious faith has nothing distinctive about it. The content itself makes a tremendous difference. The particular kinds of attitudes, convictions and commitments that permeate the life of a genuine Christian differ radically from the attitudes, convictions and commitments that permeate the life of a consistent, clearheaded unbeliever.

Furthermore, this content may correspond to equally momentous differences in the way the person relates to that content. As we noted earlier, religious beliefs have an essentially prescriptive role; they are not truly believed if the belief is merely intellectual and makes no difference in the believer's life. Furthermore—as we also noted—the special character of religious belief demands an unusually strong commitment on the part of the individual. The religious believer cannot regard her faith merely as a hypothesis to which she has a certain degree of commitment. The commitment—insofar as it constitutes a genuine faith—must be decisive and total. The believer claims that this commitment is not a "mere opinion"; it is a conviction which she holds firmly, a conviction which both stems from and underlies the existential commitment she has made.

So it is true, in one sense, that "everyone has faith." But there is a special kind of faith that is uniquely religious. Even here, however, there is a plurality. Different religions engender different types of religious faith. There is, therefore, a distinctly Christian kind of faith, though the task of describing that faith in its details falls outside the general project of philosophy of religion. The existence of this pluralism raises, once more, the question of commitment: how does one choose?

Could One Religion Be True?

The pluralism that faces the contemporary believer is most dramatically evident in the existence of competing religions. Even if we leave out varieties of secular humanism, we still have Christianity, Judaism, Islam, Hinduism and Buddhism as active faiths with millions of adherents. Is it reasonable to commit oneself to just one of these religions? Could one religion contain the final truth?

An increasing number of people feel the answer is no, for at least two reasons. First, there are concerns about tolerance and arrogance. Is it not arrogant to claim that one's own religion contains the final truth? And is not such a claim intolerant? Missionary activity and proselytizing should be replaced by dialogue and mutual respect, according to many religious thinkers. Second, the view that one religion contains the final truth seems provincial. Surely God has not limited his revelation to one geographical section or ethnic group.

Those who regard it as at least possible that all religions are true—those we might call *religious pluralists*—tend to employ one of two different strategies. We will examine each in turn. The first approach says that we should stop thinking about religious truth in propositional terms and recognize that, religiously speaking, it is personal lives that are true or false.[22] One proponent of this view tells of a Muslim he met in the Himalayas.[23] The man was selling fruit and had a primitive scale. There was no way of verifying the accuracy of the scale, but the man's honesty was sustained by a verse from the Qur'an: "Lo! He over all things is watching." The idea, on this first view, is that this verse in the Qur'an "became true" in the person's life.[24]

If this view is right, then we do not have to ask, Which religion is true? They can all be true, in the sense that they all can give rise to "true lives." To look at different religions as offering competing theories is, on this view, a mistake.

This first version of religious pluralism contains a deep insight, but the insight is accompanied by some confusion. It is quite right to stress that religious truth must be personally appropriated. In one sense of the word "true," one might appropriately speak of a person's life being true.[25] Furthermore, there is no necessary correlation between the objective truth of a proposition and the "truth" of the life of someone who accepts that proposition. It is conceivable that a person might believe objectively correct religious truths, yet personally live "falsely," because of a lack of interiorization of that truth. Furthermore, a person who believes objectively false propositions may still have some "truth" in his life, for it is possible for a person to be better than his beliefs, especially if those beliefs are mainly "intellectual assent" and have not been properly interiorized. None of this implies, however, that religions do not make competing truth claims. It is possible that one religion is objectively true, in the sense that most of its propositional claims are correct, while those of its competitors are false. Nor is this objective truth unimportant. If it is false that "Allah is watching over all things," then, in an important sense, the Himalayan fruit seller is deceived. Should he come to discover the objective falsehood of this proposition, this may affect the "truth" of his life.

Similarly, it makes no sense to say of Christianity that it has no objective truth status. If a person believes Jesus is the Son of God, it is all-important for her to interiorize this. But if Jesus is not really the Son of God, then it is a mistake for her to interiorize the belief that he is. And it is hard to see how the proposition that Jesus is the Son of God could become true for an individual merely by her accepting and appropriating it. The believer in Jesus does not believe that she has the power to make Jesus the Son of God or deny Jesus that status by her manner of believing. Rather, she believes that it is because Jesus really is the Son of God that she should believe in him and act on that belief.

The second strategy for eliminating the conflict between religions comes from John Hick. His approach differs from the first in admitting that religions do make objective truth claims and that these claims at least apparently conflict. Hick suggests, however, that the differences may be merely apparent. His basic idea is that God, "in himself," is an infinite reality "and as such transcends the grasp of the human mind."[26] Perhaps—as a popular Hindu analogy depicts it—the apparently conflicting views the various religions have developed about God are like the apparently conflicting descriptions produced by a group of blind people, each of whom felt and described a different part of the same elephant. The various religions all present "images of the divine, each expressing some aspect or range of aspects and yet none by itself fully and exhaustively corresponding to the infinite nature of the ultimate reality."[27] The apparent differences are due to the differing interpretations humans have placed on their experience of the divine, which are due to the different cultural and historical circumstances which have conditioned the experiences.[28] Hick calls for a new dialogue between the world religions on this basis, a dialogue which hopefully will resolve their apparent disagreements.

Hick's approach has much appeal. It does seem likely that the religious experiences of diverse cultures would contain true insights about God, and Hick is right to call for dialogue among the world's religions, as such dialogue—if conducted appropriately and respectfully—seems likely to yield fruitful results. A person committed to a particular faith need not regard all other faiths as completely wrong. Indeed, there may be many points of similarity, as is obviously the case with the great theistic religions.

It is doubtful that the disagreements between the world's religions can be resolved as easily as Hick suggests, however. First,

Hick's proposal implies that we must become skeptics about God, in the final analysis. We do not really know God as he is, for God as he is "transcends human thought." In what sense, then, are our human images true images of God? Is any image truer than any other? If it is equally correct to think of God, on the one hand, as a person who is capable of answering prayers and performing miracles and, on the other hand, as an impersonal reality with no will or self-consciousness, then what view of God would be incorrect? The term "God" here threatens to become so nebulous as to lose all sense.

Second, Hick's proposal is not quite what it seems. On the surface, he seems to say that all religions could be true. But what about the "exclusive" claims made by various religions? For example, Muslims claim that Muhammad is the supreme and finally authoritative prophet of God, and that the Qur'an must take preference over other revelations. It is hard to see how this Muslim claim can be reconciled with orthodox Christianity, which says that Jesus is uniquely the Son of God and that salvation comes only through him. And how can this Christian claim, in turn, be reconciled with orthodox Hindu and Buddhist views, which might admit Jesus as *a* revealer of God and *a* path to salvation, but could never admit Jesus as the *only* way and truth? There are obviously a number of claims made by various world religions that are incompatible with those made by other religions. In what follows we shall take Christian beliefs about Jesus as our illustration of this general problem.

Hick's response to the problem Christians have in reconciling their view of Jesus with what other religions say is revealing. He says that Christians must simply abandon their traditional belief in the doctrine of the incarnation. It appears, then, that it is not the case that the religions of the world are all compatible, as they stand. Rather, Hick is proposing to Christians that they modify their faith to make it compatible with other faiths.

If a person is a Christian, then whether he should be willing to modify his faith in this way depends on the grounds that he has for his faith. What is his basis for believing that Jesus is uniquely God?

Traditionally, Christians have held this conviction on the basis of their acceptance of the Bible as a special, authoritative revelation from God.

Hick's proposal draws us back to the basic issue of how one knows religious truth. If special, authoritative revelation is impossible, or if, in fact, one has never occurred, then something like Hick's view might be plausible. His position is the natural development of what was termed (in chapter five) the liberal view of revelation.[29] If, however, one holds that humankind's natural knowledge of God is inadequate, distorted by sin, and that a special revelation from God is required if we are to truly know God, then Hick's proposal will seem dubious. Hick is in effect assuming, in Pelagian fashion, the essential ability of humankind to know God and be on good terms with him.[30] If one believes that this assumption is dubious, then Hick's proposal will also appear dubious.

It is important to recognize, however, that someone who chooses to believe in the Bible as specially authoritative has not necessarily rejected reason. The questions whether a revelation could be authoritative, and, if so, whether one has occurred, can be rationally discussed. It is conceivable that reason might recognize that its ability to come to know God, operating within its natural abilities, is severely limited, and might see the need and value of a special revelation. Furthermore, reason can and must evaluate rival candidates to be such a revelation.

If someone is committed to an exclusivist religion, does this entail that he is intolerant or arrogant? We do not think so. True tolerance and respect require a recognition of genuine differences. Genuine dialogue likewise begins with a cordial admission of differences and a willingness to respect sincere disagreement.

Are there situations in which a religious believer (or unbeliever) ought to change her beliefs and convert to some other worldview? If the process of rationally testing one's faith—described earlier in this chapter—is to be more than a charade, then clearly this must be a real possibility.

A religious believer who is convinced that her faith is true is not necessarily arrogant. She can, without giving up her convictions, admit her fallibility and appreciate the perspectives of others. If she is a Christian and holds to her faith on the basis of special revelation, she cannot be arrogant. For she recognizes that the knowledge she has of God is not the result of her own cleverness but is, in fact, made possible through her recognition of her own weakness. And if she feels compelled to share her faith with others, it may not be a sign of arrogant pride or imperialism, but rather the result of a humble desire for others to know the truth.

Further Reading

The notes offer a wealth of suggestions for further reading, but the following represent those we consider especially valuable. Most of these books contain extensive bibliographies.

General Introductions

Peterson, Michael, William Hasker, Bruce Reichenbach, and David Basinger. *Reason and Religious Belief: An Introduction to the Philosophy of Religion.* 4th ed. New York: Oxford University Press, 2008.

Rowe, William L. *Philosophy of Religion: An Introduction.* 4th ed. Belmont, Calif.: Thompson/Wadsworth, 2007.

Anthologies

Peterson, Michael, William Hasker, Bruce Reichenbach, and David Basinger. *Philosophy of Religion: Selected Readings.* 3rd ed. New York: Oxford University Press, 2007.

Rowe, William L., and William J. Wainwright. *Philosophy of Religion: Selected Readings.* 3rd ed. New York: Oxford University Press, 1998.

On the Concept of God

Morris, Thomas V. *Our Idea of God: An Introduction to Philosophical Theology.* Vancouver, B.C.: Regent College Publishing, 1998.

Swinburne, Richard. *The Coherence of Theism.* Rev. ed. Oxford: Oxford University Press, 1993.

On the Theistic Arguments and Religious Experience

Alston, William P. *Perceiving God: The Epistemology of Religious Experience.* Ithaca, N.Y.: Cornell University Press, 1993.

Mavrodes, George. *Belief in God.* 1970. Reprint, Lanham, Md.: University Press of America, 1981.

Swinburne, Richard. *The Existence of God.* 2nd ed. Oxford: Clarendon, 2004.

Miracles and Special Revelation

Brown, Colin. *Miracles and the Critical Mind.* Grand Rapids: Eerdmans, 1984.

Lewis, C. S. *Miracles: A Preliminary Study.* New York: Macmillan, 1947.

Swinburne, Richard. *The Concept of Miracle.* London: Macmillan, 1970.

The Problem of Evil

Adams, Marilyn M. *Horrendous Evils and the Goodness of God.* Ithaca, N.Y.: Cornell University Press, 1999.

Adams, Robert M., and Marilyn M. Adams, eds. *The Problem of Evil.* New York: Oxford University Press, 1990.

Plantinga, Alvin. *God, Freedom, and Evil.* Grand Rapids: Eerdmans, 1977.

Faith, Reason and Commitment

Mitchell, Basil. *The Justification of Religious Belief.* Oxford: Oxford University Press, 1981.

Plantinga, Alvin, and Nicholas Wolterstorff, eds. *Faith and Rationality: Reason and Belief in God.* Notre Dame, Ind.: University of Notre Dame Press, 1983.

Plantinga, Alvin. *Warranted Christian Belief.* New York: Oxford University Press, 2000.

Notes

Chapter 1: What Is Philosophy of Religion?

[1]*Fideism*, as characterized here, is primarily a view encountered among students and ordinary religious believers. It is not meant to be a precise statement of the views of any particular theologian or philosopher. An astute reader will no doubt notice, however, that, as a general tendency, fideism has some similarity to what is sometimes termed *presuppositionalism*. Thus, views which resemble the fideist view at certain points may be found in the writings of Cornelius Van Til and Gordon Clark and, in a different theological vein, Karl Barth. The views of these men are, however, more complicated, subtle and qualified than those of any simple fideist.

It should also be noted that the term "fideism" is used in multiple ways in philosophy of religion, and many different perspectives have been described as fideistic. For an account of what is defensible in the works of some of the philosophers who are usually termed "fideists" (such as Kierkegaard), see C. Stephen Evans, *Faith Beyond Reason: A Kierkegaardian Account* (Grand Rapids: Eerdmans, 1998). In this work, Evans distinguishes what he terms "irrational fideism" (which is close to the way the term "fideism" is used in this book) from what he terms "responsible fideism," which is defended as a reasonable position.

[2]A good introduction to the theory of knowledge is the book in this series: W. Jay Wood, *Epistemology: Becoming Intellectually Virtuous* (Downers Grove, Ill.: Inter-Varsity Press, 1998).

[3]Thomas S. Kuhn, *The Structure of Scientific Revolutions,* 2nd ed. (Chicago: University of Chicago Press, 1970).

[4]See René Descartes, *Meditations on First Philosophy*, trans. Donald A. Cress, 3rd ed. (Indianapolis: Hackett, 1993).

[5]See David Hume's *An Enquiry Concerning Human Understanding* (Indianapolis: Hackett, 1977), sec. 12, p. 103.

Chapter 2: The Theistic God: The Project of Natural Theology

[1]For a good introduction to the current debate on these issues, see Thomas V. Morris, *Our Idea of God: An Introduction to Philosophical Theology* (Vancouver: Regent College Publishing, 1997). For a fine technical treatment, see Richard Swinburne, *The Coherence of Theism*, rev. ed. (Oxford: Oxford University Press, 1993).

[2]See, for example, parts 3-5 of *The Impossibility of God*, ed. Michael Martin and Ricki Monnier (Amherst, N.Y.: Prometheus, 2003).

[3]See Nelson Pike, "Divine Omniscience and Voluntary Action," *The Philosophical Review* 74 (1965): 27-46.

[4]One of the most important proposed solutions, omitted here because of the highly technical nature of the discussion, is the Ockhamist solution. Interested readers should consult the volume edited by John Martin Fischer, *God, Foreknowledge, and Freedom* (Stanford, Calif.: Stanford University Press, 1989), noting in particular the article by Alvin Plantinga, "On Ockham's Way Out."

[5]Boethius's argument is found in *The Consolation of Philosophy*; the relevant section is reprinted in *Philosophy of Religion: Selected Readings*, ed. William L. Rowe and William J. Wainwright, 3rd ed. (New York: Oxford University Press, 1998), pp. 24-32. For a contemporary defense of the Boethian solution, see T. J. Mawson, *Belief in God: An Introduction to the Philosophy of Religion* (Oxford: Clarendon Press, 2005), p. 41.

[6]The following objection is adopted from Hugh McCann, "Divine Providence," §3, in the online *Stanford Encyclopedia of Philosophy* <http://plato.stanford.edu/entries/providence-divine/#GodKnoFut>.

[7]Theological compatibilism enjoys a prominent place in the history of orthodox Christianity, being endorsed, in various forms, by Augustine, Luther, Calvin and Jonathan Edwards, among others.

[8]The claim is sometimes put in terms of the agent's choices rather than desires. The claim is then that the agent is free whenever it is true of her that *if* she had chosen otherwise, she would have done otherwise. This is sometimes called "the hypothetical sense of being able to do otherwise."

[9]See Paul Helm, "The Augustinian-Calvinist View," in *Divine Foreknowledge: Four Views*, ed. James K. Beilby and Paul R. Eddy (Downers Grove, Ill.: InterVarsity Press, 2001).

[10]For an excellent introduction to the Molinist solution, see William Lane Craig, "The Middle-Knowledge View," in *Divine Foreknowledge: Four Views,* ed. James K. Beilby and Paul R. Eddy (Downers Grove, Ill.: InterVarsity Press, 2001).

[11]The seminal critique of middle knowledge is Robert M. Adams's essay, "Middle Knowledge and the Problem of Evil," in *The Problem of Evil*, ed. Robert M. Adams and Marilyn M. Adams (Oxford: Oxford University Press, 1990).

[12]Gregory A. Boyd argues that, in addition to solving the foreknowledge problem, open theism is the *biblical* view. See "The Open-Theism View," in *Divine Foreknowledge: Four Views,* ed. James K. Beilby and Paul R. Eddy (Downers Grove, Ill.: InterVarsity Press, 2001).

[13]A. J. Ayer, *Language, Truth and Logic* (New York: Dover, 1946), pp. 115-16.

[14]For discussions of the many attempts (and failures) to develop a plausible version of the verifiability theory, see Carl G. Hempel, "The Empiricist Criterion of Meaning," in *Logical Positivism,* ed. A. J. Ayer (1959; reprint, Westport, Conn.: Greenwood Press, 1978), pp. 108-29, also printed under the title "Problems and Changes in the Empiricist Criterion of Meaning," in *Semantics and the Philosophy of Language,* ed. Leonard Linsky (Urbana: University of Illinois Press, 1952), pp. 163-85; see also Alvin Plantinga, *God and Other Minds* (Ithaca, N.Y.: Cornell University Press, 1967), pp. 156-68.

[15]See Kai Nielsen, *An Introduction to the Philosophy of Religion* (New York: St. Martin's Press, 1982), esp. pp. 18-19 and chapter six.

[16]The following section, particularly as it appeared in the first edition, is indebted to George Mavrodes's *Belief in God* (New York: Random House, 1970), pp. 17-48.

[17]Taken from Philip L. Quinn's "Divine Command Theory," in *The Blackwell Guide to Ethical Theory*, ed. Hugh LaFollette (Malden, Mass.: Blackwell, 2000), p. 66.

[18]Commenting on the argument, Quinn suggests that what is wrong with the argument is that "the second premise cannot have, apart from the argument, more epistemic justification than the conclusion, in which case the argument cannot, as a successful proof must, transmit epistemic justification from its premises to its conclusion" (ibid.).

Chapter 3: Classical Arguments for God's Existence

[1]Anselm's *Proslogion* is available in a number of editions. The crucial sections on the ontological argument are found in chapters two and three and are included in many anthologies in philosophy of religion, including the excellent one edited by William L. Rowe and William J. Wainwright, *Philosophy of Religion: Selected Readings*, 3rd ed. (New York: Oxford University Press, 1998), pp. 95-96.

[2]See Norman Malcolm, "Anselm's Ontological Arguments," *Philosophical Review* (January 1960): 41-62, reprinted in John Hick, ed., *The Existence of God* (New York: Macmillan, 1964), pp. 47-70.

[3]See Alvin Plantinga, *God, Freedom, and Evil* (Grand Rapids: Eerdmans, 1977), p. 112.

[4]See Karl Barth, *Anselm: Fides Quaerens Intellectum,* trans. Ian Robertson (Richmond, Va.: John Knox Press, 1960). Key selections from this work can be found in *The Many-Faced Argument,* ed. John Hick and Arthur C. McGill (New York: Macmillan, 1967), pp. 119-61.

[5]Actually, some philosophers make a distinction between first-cause arguments and cosmological arguments. This distinction is not particularly helpful, though. Usually, the distinction is really between two different kinds of cosmological arguments employing different concepts of causality.

[6]See Richard Taylor, *Metaphysics*, 4th ed. (Englewood Cliffs, N.J.: Prentice Hall, 1992), pp. 99-116, and Richard Swinburne, *The Existence of God*, 2nd ed. (Oxford: Oxford University Press, 2004), pp. 133-52.

[7]See William Lane Craig, *The Kalam Cosmological Argument* (London: Macmillan, 1979). A shorter and more accessible introduction to the argument is found in J. P. Moreland and William Lane Craig, *Philosophical Foundations for a Christian Worldview* (Downers Grove, Ill.: InterVarsity Press, 2003), pp. 463-81.

[8]See Stuart Hackett, *The Resurrection of Theism* (Grand Rapids: Baker, 1982), pp. 293-95, for an example of the denial of an actual infinite temporal series. The historical roots of this view have been traced by Craig in *The Kalam Cosmological Argument.* Craig also defends the argument against various objections.

[9]See William Hasker, *Metaphysics* (Downers Grove, Ill.: InterVarsity Press, 1983), pp. 116-17, for an example of the claim that the big bang theory supports theism. (Also see Hasker's footnote for additional reading on the subject.)

[10]There is a way for the critic of the cosmological argument to avoid this conclusion, but it leads to a different problem. One could contend that there are no necessary beings (including bits of matter), but insist that it is impossible for nothing to exist. The critic could claim, in other words, that everything which exists—or could possibly exist—is contingent, but it is necessary that *some* contingent being(s) or other exist. To illustrate the idea, suppose that there were only three fundamental "bits" of matter in the universe: A, B and C. The critic's view is that there is a possible way the world could have been in which A, B and C do not exist: in that scenario, D, E and F exist, perhaps. Since it is possible for A, B and C not to exist, these (the fundamental constituents of the actual world) are not necessary beings. But the critic further insists that there could not possibly have been *nothing*—i.e., that it is necessary that *something* exist, although everything which exists, or could possibly exist, is contingent. The solution thus avoids any semblance of pantheism, while still providing an answer to the question Why is there something rather than nothing? (The answer: It is impossible for there to be nothing.) Unfortunately for the critic, however, the view faces a different problem. The critic must now produce some compelling argument for the claim that it is *impossible* that there should be no contingent beings (no bits of matter)—a claim which otherwise seems highly implausible. Why should we accept that the world could not possibly have been completely void, containing no matter at all? If the critic cannot produce a compelling argument for this claim, then her objection can be dismissed. The problem, though, is that no such argument seems forthcoming. There appears to be no good reason for thinking that some matter must exist—unless, of course, one believes that the matter that actually exists is *necessarily existent:* precisely the view, discussed in the main text, which leads to pantheism.

[11]For a comprehensive treatment and defense of this principle, see Alexander R. Pruss, *The Principle of Sufficient Reason: A Reassessment* (New York: Cambridge University Press, 2006).

[12]See Paul Edwards, "The Cosmological Argument," *Rationalist Annual* (1959): 63-77, reprinted in the first edition of Rowe and Wainwright, eds., *Philosophy of Religion*, pp. 136-48.

[13]See Albert Camus, "An Absurd Reasoning," in *The Myth of Sisyphus and Other Essays* (New York: Random House, 1955), pp. 3-48.

[14]See Taylor, *Metaphysics*, pp. 109-15, Swinburne, *The Existence of God*, pp. 153-91, and F. R. Tennant, *Philosophical Theology* (Cambridge: Cambridge University Press, 1928-1930).

[15]Thomas Aquinas's "Five Ways" are found in his *Summa Theologica* 1.2.3. This section is included in numerous anthologies. The quotation here is taken from Rowe and Wainwright, eds., *Philosophy of Religion*, p. 128. An inexpensive edition of the *Summa* is available from Image Books, general editor, Thomas Gilby.

[16]Though both employ a kind of probabilistic reasoning, it is important not to confuse inference to the best explanation with inductive reasoning, discussed in chapter two.

[17]David Hume, *Dialogues Concerning Natural Religion,* ed. Norman Kemp Smith (Indianapolis: Bobbs-Merrill, 1947), pp. 148-50.

[18]Ibid., pp. 146, 174.

[19]Ibid., pp. 182-85.